RUNNING
THE
GAUNTLET

RUNNING
THE
GAUNTLET

ESSENTIAL BUSINESS LESSONS
TO LEAD, DRIVE CHANGE,
AND GROW PROFITS

JEFFREY W. HAYZLETT
WITH JIM EBER

NEW YORK   CHICAGO   SAN FRANCISCO
LISBON   LONDON   MADRID   MEXICO CITY   MILAN
NEW DELHI   SAN JUAN   SEOUL   SINGAPORE
SYDNEY   TORONTO

1 2 3 4 5 6 7 8 9 10   DOC/DOC   1 6 5 4 3 2 1

ISBN 978-0-07-178409-2
MHID   0-07-178409-8

e-ISBN 978-0-07-178410-8
e-MHID   0-07-178410-1

Book design by Lee Fukui and Mauna Eichner

McGraw-Hill products are available at special quantity discounts to use as premiums and sales promotions or for use in corporate training programs. To contact a representative, please e-mail us at bulksales@mcgraw-hill.com.

This book is printed on acid-free paper.

To all the naysayers, opportunists, and obstructionists who do their best to stop the progress of change in an organization. Note: we will beat you.

Contents

Think Big: Attitude Adjustments

Acknowledgments

In *The Mirror Test*, I acknowledged all the really important people in my life. They know who they are, and I continue to cherish them for letting me be me. So let me thank a few others who made this book possible.

To Jim, my writer and fellow bacon-loving friend, for helping make sense of the jumble of thoughts that dart within my head. To Wendy Keller of Keller Media, Inc., for being one of the toughest people in business; nobody could have a better agent or a better friend. To Mary Glenn, my editor, for turning us loose and giving us the needed direction from time to time. And to the team at McGraw-Hill for elevating this book to the places it needs to be!

And most important, to all the team members and employees at all the companies I have worked with over the years: thank you for letting me hone the craft and drive the change—I loved every minute of it! Let's do it again; it's time to saddle up and ride!

About the SnapTag

Snap this tag to interact with me at every chapter! *Running the Gauntlet* is about driving change in your organization. I chose to add mobile activation to this book to avail myself of the transformative opportunity to connect with you, the reader, as well as to support what we feel are important concepts and practices for any company out there, connecting with the people who buy, use, and evangelize products and services—yours and ours.

SnapTags are found at the beginning of each chapter. The SnapTags offer a direct link to related video content explaining the core concepts featured in each chapter.

There are two options for activating the SnapTag:

1. Snap and send: Take a photo of the SnapTag and send it via picture message (mms) to 77865, or e-mail gauntlet@snaptag.mobi.

2. Scan the SnapTag with the SnapTag Reader available at the Android Market or iPhone App Store when you search for "SnapTag Reader."

I hope you enjoy the added interactivity the SnapTags provide while reading *Running the Gauntlet*.

Happy Snapping

To learn more about SnapTags visit www.spyderlynk.com.

Driving change in business can feel like running the gauntlet *every day*: threatening, hostile, and scary—and the only way to survive.

We were meeting in that conference room again—*the* conference room, the one with the clock on the wall that had been wrong for months and that annoyed everyone in the room, including me. But I wasn't about to change it myself.

Okay, I'm sure it seems strange to start a book about change with a story about *refusing* to change something, but bear with me.

You see, I *could* have changed the time. I'm 6'3". I could have just reached up, opened the face, and moved the hands. But I wasn't just annoyed at the clock anymore. I had decided to wait and see how long it would take for someone else in the room to act once everyone became aware of the problem. After all, a crucial first step in implementing change is being aware there *is* a problem. And sure enough, the team became aware. Every single time my team had a meeting in that conference room, someone now said, "That clock is off. I wish someone would change it." But then I listened in amazement as the team just talked how to do it to death.

This time, after one too many discussions about why the clock was off, how to approach it, and how to go about requisitioning a change from Building Services, I had had enough. I challenged them. "Who has the guts to change it? Why doesn't one of you just get up there and change the clock and get it done rather than talking and waiting for someone else in the company to fix it?"

Finally, one of them said, "You're right." She pulled a chair over, climbed up, and moved the hands. Done.

That's how change in business gets started: someone sees a need, takes the challenge personally, and acts. And that clock story sums up the problem with change, too: it takes too long for people to see the need and even longer for them to act—or for leaders to determine who should take action and motivate them to do it. Too often, we all need a push.

I believe most leaders and employees know when their old ways of doing business must change or their businesses will die, yet they don't act. They have the ability to enact big changes, but too often they just don't. Maybe they can't see what needs to be done. Maybe they are scared of mistakes or failure. Maybe they refuse to hold themselves accountable and take responsibility. Maybe change seems too hard, and they are too tired. But change won't ever come passively through attrition, delegation, or waiting around for someone else to take responsibility. That's not fogging the mirror; you're already dead or dying.

So, how do you learn to act like an agent of change? How do you get your employees to buy into the changes you need? How do you change your business in a charismatic, effective way that instills enthusiasm and results in profits? The same way I do: you get up in your business. If something sucks, get rid of it. If it isn't working, change it and own those changes. Refuse to tolerate problems and passivity. Period.

That's easier said than done, though. I know this ride is not easy to start or sustain. That's why I say that change in business is like "running the gauntlet." In real life, that was not a game—at least, not one any frontier cowboy ever wanted to play. Running the gauntlet was a form of extreme physical torture exacted on prisoners by some Native American tribes. When the braves captured a cowboy or a settler, they would take him back to camp, strip him to the waist, and drag him to the front of a path lined on each side by the members of the tribe (the *whole* tribe), with each member being armed with sticks, stones, clubs, or whatever else they had that would hurt . . . badly. The channel of angry tribesmen was the real gauntlet the captive had to run as everyone tried to beat him. And that was just to get a head start before the tribesmen took their horses and hunted him down.

Are you ready? Go!

For business leaders, being on the frontier of change every day feels like you're running the gauntlet. A threatening and hostile environment surrounds you on all sides. Your business life depends on your stamina and survival skills—and your ability to absorb some serious body blows. Like the cavalry of old, even when you *have* all the troops, permissions, strategies, and tools of change, even when you prepare and project well, you will run a gauntlet of saboteurs inside and out. It's more than just market shifts, instant trends, and the wild ride of the stock markets. It's the people who work against (and even for) you. People everywhere always feel they have the right to challenge you, strike at you, and try to hurt or even kill your business. Naysayers, opportunists, obstructionists, and even partners and employees will balk, bicker, and fight. They will let you down, and others will try to destroy you, both covertly and overtly. All this on top of the challenge of getting yourself motivated to see your changes all the way through to success.

Are you really ready? Go!

I'm ready. As you'll hear me say throughout the book: at least when you're running the gauntlet in business, no one is going to die. So, as I like to say, "Cowboy up or go sit in the truck!" Let's run the gauntlet and develop a "takeover mentality" for your business together. Let's look at the clock face of your business and act. Let's really get up in your business and summon the vision, courage, and passion to take it over from the inside and drive some change. Let's hone the mental, emotional, and (yes) physical toughness you must have if you are to create smart, strategic, and lasting change. And then let's tackle the actual implementation of that change and deal with any disruptions it will cause. Finally, let's discuss how to create and sustain momentum and learn how to adapt or die. This book takes you through all these steps in short chapters with tweetable titles that really zero in on each step in thinking big and growing bigger.

But listen carefully: I may be a change cowboy from the plains of South Dakota with size 12 cowboy boots that can kick some serious business butt, but I am not about using force for force's sake. Bull in a china shop approaches to change in business, just like a stampede on the trail, do not lead to long-term solutions. They get you there, but at what cost? Smart cowboys know never to hit their horses to get them to do something—the only thing it does is hurt your hands. I have a horse I call Glue ('cause that's what he's gonna be some day). Glue's great, but he doesn't like to do even the easy things, like saddling up. He bites and jumps and runs around and generally just makes everything hard. So, I give him a choice. First, I let him run the way he wants in the pen. As he runs, I pester him—just enough to make him uncomfortable but not make him angry or hurt him—but soon I stop and call him over, tell him he is a good boy, and stroke his head. I then repeat the process until Glue realizes that doing what he wants to do is difficult and the best thing to do is to change and do it my way.

Like my approach with Glue, change in business works best when it is both tough *and* thoughtful. Small or big business is bad only if you are not changing and thinking big to grow bigger!

Let's ride!

Friendsourcing Change

As part of the preparation of this book, I turned to some of the smartest people I know (who are the people I know) and asked them to answer some broad questions about being agents of change. I didn't just crowdsource; I friendsourced, which to me is a more important and effective trend of the last few years. Crowdsourcing is a cool tool for spot surveys, quick answers, and general engagement, but friendsourcing is about trust—reaching out to your most valued advisors (the people you really know) and finding out what they think. You'll find these answers and my comments on them in complementing chapters throughout this book.

Part One

Think
Big

Attitude
Adjustments

Repeat after me: no one is going to die from the changes you make in business. Say it: "No. One. Is. Going. To. Die."

I had just sat down to dine with some business friends at an upscale Chinese restaurant in San Francisco when the waiters set down finger bowls in front of us, each with a little floating flower.

The friend who was sitting next to me looked at the flower and then asked, "Jeff, I get the finger bowls, but are you supposed to eat the flower?"

"I don't know," I said. It looked harmless enough. "I guess you can."

My friend had no sooner put the flower in his mouth when the Chinese maître d' rushed over, waving his hands and yelling in broken English, "No, no, no, no! Decoration! For decoration!"

My friend spit out the flower and looked horrified. We laughed for a moment, and then I noticed that the flower had turned my friend's tongue black.

"Dude, look at your tongue! It's black!"

"What?" My friend grabbed a mirror and looked at his tongue. "Oh my God! Oh my God! My tongue is black! Do you think I've been poisoned? Do you think it's poisonous? Will it kill me?"

The maître d' rushed over. He looked down gravely at my friend, who looked up in sheer terror.

The maître d' paused. "No die. Little sick maybe, but no die."

My friend was fine that night, and guess what? You will be too. So, before we go any further, remember: no one is going to die when running this gauntlet. Not you. Not your employees. No one. Little sick maybe, but no die.

Yet still, as you start to make the changes you need, you will think, "People are going to die." But they aren't. So don't think that. Your *business* might die. But that's probably because it already was not breathing well.

Yes, if you are in manufacturing, please: safety first. If you are making lifesaving equipment, please do not cut corners and ignore important details while you are executing change. I don't want to hear anyone saying, "Jeff Hayzlett told me no one was going to die, so I didn't check the defibrillator."

The truth is, businesses that aren't checking their defibrillators are *not* changing; they are cutting corners and hoping they can survive. Change is not about being irresponsible, reckless, or careless. And while lives are not at stake, livelihoods are. If you are not successful, jobs will be lost. Mortgages and retirement and college funds will be affected. This is not a game. Driving change is about driving success, and it is serious. You know that. You're playing with your reputation, and your future, too. Or you'd better be. Otherwise, please put this down and give it to someone I can respect.

I mean it. Good economy? Bad economy? It doesn't matter. I am sick and tired of people acting scared, whining about all the things they can't do, thinking through every little detail, and then playing it safe. That's the path to mediocrity, and it makes change agents miserable. Heck, it makes everyone miserable. You may *think* you need to play it safe so you don't "lose." But you don't ever *know* what's going to work. And so what! Please, tell me: what's the worst that's gonna happen? You make a mistake? People point fingers? You lose a client? You lose some money? You lose your job? Maybe. Most likely, the worst you will get is a paper cut—literally and figuratively.

In the end, most businesses can sustain a little "ready, fire, aim" when they're changing. If you want to test something out, go for it. Think it through, but take risks. Push like crazy, and be persistent. That's the mental edge you need. One mistake or setback does not mean total failure. Seven out of every ten things change agents do will be good, and three will fall flat. Those are good odds. Be strong as you run the gauntlet.

You'll need that strength to overcome your fear—and let's face it: this is scary. In order to enact change, you need to create tension. Causing tension is the foundation of the change agent's no-one-is-going-to-die attitude. You walk around all the time asking, "What can we change? What can we do to make it *better*?" Having trouble getting started? Do what change agents like me do: look for change everywhere you go. Go to a restaurant you love or a business you admire and ask yourself, what do you think it could do better? Then turn that same spotlight on yourself and your business.

But don't wait for every change to happen before you start selling it. Remember, no one is going to die. Sometimes you need to put things out there and move a little faster than you are actually moving. Or, as I like to say: put a stake far enough out.

Think of this like a business version of what *Survivorman*'s Les Stroud does to film his TV show. Les goes it alone in the woods for seven days with no food and no shelter. Yes, *alone*. Unlike the people on other knockoff shows, Les brings his own camera. There's no crew. No gimmicks. So, how does he film it?

He actually walks to where he wants to shoot, plants the camera, walks back to where he started, and then walks back to the camera.

Leaders need to do this metaphorically. For example, Kodak did this in 2006 when the wonderful Carl Gustin, whom I succeeded as CMO, created a brilliant four-minute video called "Winds of Change" (Google Kodak + "Winds of Change") to tell customers about the company's transformation from analog to digital. Watch it. Were all the changes mentioned in the video already in place? Heck, no. But Carl was putting a stake in the ground for everyone to see. (Kodak and other companies still use this video today.)

And what did I do after I took over from Carl as CMO? I changed it.

I realized the video was perfect for consumers, but we needed a different version for Kodak's rapidly growing business-to-business side, which was dominated by white males. Our editors knew this. Not only did they change the content, but they changed the language, using more colorful expressions—none more so than when the actor on stage gestured at his crotch and said Kodak had "big brass *cojones*."

I love to cause tension, but that raised even *my* eyebrows.

When I screened the video for my team members, most of them women, I asked if it passed the "female filter" for crassness. They loved it. I took their word for it and let it fly. Maybe I should have run it through the Hispanic female filter, not just the female filter, because the feedback was immediate: mostly positive from the customers, but negative from a few media people and bloggers and a bunch of people inside the company who found it crude and unfunny . . . including my CEO. My *Spanish* CEO.

Imagine getting *that* call after being on the job for a couple of weeks. I was thinking, "I'm gonna get fired." I felt like throwing up as I headed to his office.

"Jeff . . . do you know the meaning of the word *cojones*?" he asked. (I was sure at that moment that I didn't in full.) "In Spanish, *cojones* is *the crudest description* of the male anatomy."

You can't worry about setbacks like this as a change agent. If you believe it is the right thing to do, you must stand behind what you do and really push to the edge of the table.

And sometimes you don't know you have pushed things *off* the edge of the table until they *hit the floor*. I changed the video overnight. It is now a legend—a lightning bolt for representing change.

And no one died.

Chapter 2

Change begins by changing the questions. Who would want a horseless carriage? Wrong question. The right one: Why wouldn't everyone want one?

Imagine you're living in the 1890s. The dominant transportation technology is the horse. Almost anyone who needs one has one. People know how to take care of horses and to either saddle them up for a one-off ride or hitch them to a surrey, wagon, or buggy. If you live in the country, you turn them loose and they pretty much feed themselves. You can get a horse in any "make," "model," color, and style you want. You could even get a compact one in pony size.

Then, along comes a radical, newfangled idea: the "horseless carriage." But why would people want to change what they have? Why would anyone want a horseless carriage?

"Who would want a horseless carriage?" That's the wrong question. The right ones are: "Why *wouldn't* you want one? Why would anyone want to put up with the limitations, piles of manure, and inconveniences of the current way of doing things?'"

People needed to be reminded of all the inconvenient things about horses. They need food all the time. You've got to clean up after them, and have you ever seen and smelled what comes out of the back end of a horse? Plus, you need hours to get a horse ready. It needs shelter and pampering. (I hear that today, people even pay for a kind of coin-operated massage for their horses. Next time someone wants to spend money for a coin-op horse massage, call me. But I digress.)

Consumers needed to be reminded of the pain-in-the-butt parts of what they had gotten used to in order to see how the horseless carriage did away with those inconveniences. It offered seemingly unlimited possibilities for growth and prosperity. Were there new problems to go with those possibilities? Sure. Affordability, reliability, tires, where to get gas ... the early manufacturers and adopters faced all these problems and more.

But that's not a problem for Americans. We jump to respond to this kind of change. We're what the economist Amar Bhidé, in *The Venturesome Economy: How Innovation Sustains Prosperity in a More Connected World* (Princeton, N.J.: Princeton University Press, 2010), calls "venturesome consumers." He defines "venturesome consumption" as our "willingness and ability ... to effectively use products and technologies derived from scientific research." We don't fear innovation and change. We long to consume it. We were ready for those horseless carriages—if someone could just make enough of them and make them affordable and reliable enough.

As Bhidé notes, American businesses are venturesome, too. Certainly this was true of the father of the mass-produced horseless carriage: Henry Ford, a gifted engineer. After his Detroit Automobile Company failed, Ford continued designing and building cars, and in 1902, he cofounded Ford Motor Company. While other companies produced cars that were like expensive works of art, Ford saw another way: the assembly line, which made it possible for less-skilled workers to turn out more cars than any of his rivals. Productivity was so astounding that Ford stopped measuring it. By 1914, other companies needed five times as many workers to build the same hundreds of thousands of cars as Ford. Ford also developed incredible supply chain efficiencies to complement the assembly line, even having parts shipped in boxes that could be repurposed as floorboards. He turned the economic practice of the time on its head by doubling the wages and reducing the workweek of his loyal employees so that they could buy cars and have the time to drive them. Put another way, he slashed his profit per unit in order to sell more cars.

Ford's Model T thus became the car almost anyone could afford, and America's car culture was born. The car became the thing people *needed*. Ford had speed, reliability, lower cost, and profit. Venturesome consumption, indeed. Driving change.

Until the next time venturesome becomes fearful. (After all, someone first put a saddle on a horse, too. Imagine being the first person to ever ride a wild horse.) Until intrepid and innovative become comfortable and cautious. Until we fall back on our success instead of adapting and changing to build new futures.

The truth is, we get used to what we have and grow numb to our processes, procedures, and ways of doing things (especially if the profits are still good). Essentially, we resign ourselves to mediocrity. But like taking care of those horses, mediocrity is a lot of work. Mountains and mountains of crap blind you to the fact that someone else is innovating—doing things better, faster, and cheaper than you. Your business may look like it's breathing and fogging the mirror, but as I said in *The Mirror Test*, you'll look good in your coffin, too.

Change agents have to ask venturesome questions: why would anyone want to put up with the limitations, crap, and inconveniences of the current way of doing things?

If I had worked at Motorola, I might tell tales of the first wireless phones that we carried in bags over our shoulders. But I worked at Kodak. I had it worse. I worked at a company that makes *film*. When I did sales and marketing presentations, I'd ask an audience of thousands, "How many of you have bought a roll of film in the past year?" One or two hands would go up. (I'd be sure to thank them for helping us.) Then I'd ask, "How many of you own a digital camera or a smartphone with a camera?" Every hand would go up. "Welcome to my world," I'd say.

You think you have sales and marketing problems? Kodak went from $15 billion to a couple of hundred million in film. Unlike, say, Cisco, which killed its popular Flip camera when it saw the writing on the iPhone, Kodak was like so many others: a victim of its own hubris and single-minded focus on what it had done well for so long. Ultimately, mama did not take your Kodachrome away; our customers did. They stopped buying it. Most photographers went digital. A few migrated to other Kodak films. After 73 years and tons of technological upgrades, the bestselling film of all time made up less than 1 percent of Kodak's declining film business and was retired in 2009.

How different might Kodak's fortunes be today if it had stayed venturesome, changed the question, and acted on one possibility that was literally right in front of it—the digital camera? Kodak actually invented it in 1975. Revolutionary. Way ahead of its time. The trouble is, if you had asked an audience in 1975, "Who has bought a roll of film in the past month?" every hand would have gone up. That meant big money—why change? As a result, Kodak never held a perceived dominant position in the digital camera market of the future.

I arrived at Kodak at a time when the company was trying to change in a way that was absolutely necessary but was radically different from its established ways of doing business. A full 60 percent of the people were like me: recent hires. Kodak had invested billions in new technologies and acquiring new companies to speed its transformation from an analog consumer-oriented company to a digital business-to-business-oriented one. Revenue growth from those businesses quickly outstripped that from the established consumer businesses. By 2008, 19 products—all among the top three in their field—accounted for 80 percent of our revenue, and half of them had not existed four years before.

While I was at Kodak, the *Financial Times* said that in a decade, the Kodak story could be considered one of the great financial turnarounds. I hope that is right. As I write this book, things for the company continue to be tough financially; driving change can't always undo years (in this case decades) of ignoring the need for that change. At the very least, we bought a great American brand more time.

I wish that what I learned from all the financial, technological, cultural, operational, and strategic changes at Kodak could provide a simple road map for changes at any company. But it can't. You think you will have a tough time changing? You're right. Old and new will clash. Things will not work, and systems will break down. You will fail and make mistakes. It will be messy. Even for experienced change agents, "change" is easy to say and hard to do.

Nobody wishes to have these messy things happen, but change agents still need to stand up and say, "What we are doing now is not right, and I'm going to change it." Those changes are the path to seeing your markets and your customers in new ways—a chance to consider new strategies and possibilities, investigate and invest in new technologies, bring in new and different people, invent new ways of doing business, test things, and more. And great leaders take on these challenges by being

- Problem solvers, not problem seekers

- Change agents for the processes

- Cheerleaders who reinforce goals

- Seam operators

We'll get to all of these shortly, but now you've learned how to get started: by seeing that the established way is rife with negatives and change is full of opportunities. You've learned to change the question.

Fear stops most people. Change agents welcome it. Get past your fear. Act with confidence and be willing to be a beginner.

Alot of people think that my Sioux Falls address and awesome cowboy boots mean I've been a cowboy all my life. Let me shatter that image right now: I am not a cowboy. I wasn't one when I was growing up, and I never wanted to be one. I grew up on military bases (my dad was in the Air Force), not the plains, and while I live in South Dakota now, I do not live on a ranch. I like Westerns, but I prefer war movies. I always wanted a horse; I just never had the money to buy and keep one. And when I got to my forties and finally could afford one, I'd love to tell you I knew instinctively what to do. I'd love to, but I'd be lying.

The truth is, I learned how to saddle my first horse from a 14-year-old girl. She had the experience, *and* I was willing to look, listen, and learn from her and be a beginner.

Yeah, I could have been cocky and pretended to know everything. I'm Jeffrey Hayzlett, the global business celebrity! I've faced bigger challenges than this girl or anyone else will ever see! I've seen horses and watched movies and even been to a few dude ranches where we all rode together and got led in a circle! How different could this be? Very . . . and I knew that. I was willing to get over myself and be a beginner.

Being a beginner does not mean being unprepared. Before I met my saddle sister, I did what any twenty-first-century cowboy wannabe would do: I got *Horses for Dummies*, Googled "owning horses," and read everything I could. I watched videos. I visited friends who had horses. I bought a saddle and a trailer to get my horse home (which I soon learned is an adventure in itself). And finally, on a cold March day, my son and I hitched up the trailer and drove north of Sioux Falls to get our horse and bring him back to where we would board him.

That's where I met the girl who showed me how to saddle my horse, and out I went. Not with a "Hi-ho Silver and away!" but more of a "Whoa! Whoa! [Shiver] Stay!" I still needed help getting out on the trail, and I had no idea what else was in store. A few *years* later, I'm a good rider, and my love for my horses is bigger than anything else except my love for my family. I can trailer my horses, give them shots, and know when they are going to buck. But what would have happened if I had been afraid of being a beginner? I'd never have mastered my own horses, and I would not have been able to face and handle any of the countless horses I've ridden since.

Today, no horse scares me enough to stop me from climbing aboard. But with every new horse, I still take the time to look, listen, and learn, because while it is hardly my first time riding, it is my first time on that ride. I don't want to make a dumb mistake by assuming I know more than I do. The most easygoing of these magnificent animals could throw me from the saddle at any time, no matter how prepared I am.

In *The Mirror Test*, I talked about being a beginner in terms of value and marketing. I called it "winning before you begin," and I showed my thought process by going through the 20 questions

I always ask before launching a project (see Appendix A). When I was reviewing some old presentations, I found this list for competitive change:

1. Know your conditions of satisfaction.

2. Have a winning attitude—get over your fear and be a beginner.

3. Know your business and the business of good management.

4. Have enough money and capital to move ahead.

5. Pay attention to details.

6. Build a team that can succeed.

7. Manage your time better—get out of the way and delegate.

8. Have the tools to complete the job you promised.

9. Keep the customer satisfied with your quality and responsiveness.

10. Compete smartly and power through on your promises.

It's pretty basic, but that's the point! Circumstances may change, but the attitude leaders must have when they're driving change through a business doesn't. You stand in the way of a winning attitude when you refuse to stretch yourself to be a beginner. You'll go into everything thinking you know the answers. All that does is prevent leaders from being surprised by what the answers will be. And I want to be surprised. I like being surprised. Being a beginner simply means, "I have experience. I have confidence. But I admit I don't know everything, and this [company, project, team] is new to me." Be a blank slate and listen, look, and learn. Ask stupid questions and know that it is okay. No one is going to die.

Being willing to be a beginner is how you get past your "three seconds of fear." Three seconds: that's the difference between doing something and not doing it. And change agents welcome those three seconds. Feeling that fear means we are embarking on something great. But we must get over those three seconds, because the gauntlet of change is scary enough to look down. We are facing big problems with huge challenges, and we know that we cannot and will not always succeed. Fear only gets in the way.

That includes a fear of those who disagree with us and can help define that change through healthy debate. Our increasingly one-sided political culture has infected many of us with a desire to listen only to people who agree with us, as if listening to the other side and engaging it is a sign of weakness. Actually, the opposite is true, especially in business. I know tons of people who run great businesses but are lousy change agents because they are single-minded asses—total jerks who eat up their people and those who disagree with them. Sometimes these jerks win, but not over the long haul. Good change agents string a lot of great successes together. Healthy debate pushes us to better define our principles and consider new possibilities. It shouldn't make leaders doubt what they are doing.

After all, leaders learn quickly that many of the changes they seek won't be right the first time (beginner's luck notwithstanding). That's the first test of this attitude: adjust and try to be better, or stop and say that we tried that and it did not work. When I started playing rugby, my team didn't know anything. We lost our first game 80–0. The other team made fun of us. It was awful. But none of us walked away. We realized that we were still learning and we needed to adjust. For example, I learned just how slow I was that first game: they measured my speed with a calendar. So

I took a different approach: I played up my size and gave dastardly and aggressive looks. I growled and beat my head on the ground. I pretended I was a buffalo and gnawed at the grass. I did everything to convince them I was crazy. And the first guy still crushed me. But I stuck with it and resolved along with the team to get it right or be mediocre at best. We won that game.

That's what a winning attitude and a willingness to be a beginner is all about. But if you notice, as is sometimes the case with me, I just stepped in number two on my old list! We still need to attack number one.

Friendsourcing Being Grounded

Jim Collins cautioned us to avoid the hubris of our own success: don't be too rigid or too steadfastly tied to the way it's always been and fail to think about the way it is going to be. To me, avoiding this mistake comes down to one word, *awareness*, and awareness comes down to one of my favorite expressions: admitting you don't know what you don't know. When I walk around New York City, where I now live part of the time, I'm still a big kid from South Dakota. I get excited when I walk outside every day, and I can't believe I get to do what I do with so many great people and companies. That's what being a beginner is about for me—that's what keeps me grounded and constantly aware: the joy of discovering what I don't know every day! And I try to stay in that sense of awareness in everything I do, excited and unafraid to be a beginner. I walk in with an ego and then let it go.

Be like this and maybe you can avoid what Dina Kaplan, the cofounder of blip.tv, told me she did wrong when her company launched: "We thought we had this great product, and we just thrust it on our users and said, 'Here you go!' We should have paused, listened to the influencers in our world, built up friendships and trust, and then asked: 'What do you think of this product we've been working on? How can we improve it?' You don't enter a conversation by yelling at people; you enter it by pausing and listening and only then, after some time, speaking up." Joe Pulizzi, a content marketing evangelist and "lover of all things orange," made the same mistake: "I fell in love with the idea of our product. Not that it was a bad product, but it just wasn't needed in the industry as much as I thought. I sought out advice from my mentors too late in the process. They saw this coming way before I did. If I had a do-over, I would have talked to my mentors at least every other month instead of about every six months."

Ann M. Devine, executive director of Pi Sigma Epsilon (the national sales and marketing fraternity), echoes both of these change agents: "In all the companies I worked with and for, they all had one thing in common: whether they were a small business or Fortune 1000, at some point they forgot about the basics. Simple things like segmenting markets, increasing revenues and decreasing expenses, or thinking marketing was creating brochures and catalogs."

Overconfidence, arrogance, forgetting the basics . . . three of the deadliest sins that leaders commit when they fail to check in constantly and forget the basic rules of testing and trying things out before they go. In other words, "kids," take our advice: do your homework and ground yourself in the processes, data, and marketing expertise you need if you are to succeed.

Chapter 4

As Churchill said, "There is nothing wrong with change if it is in the right direction." Know your conditions of satisfaction.

I think many companies' best days are ahead of them. Thinking from that perspective, you can change a lot of things as a leader and grow bigger. But you'll start badly or lose your way if you fail to obey this simple piece of wisdom: don't go in if you don't know the way out. That's what conditions of satisfaction help you do: find your way into and out of change. They define what your mission is and where you want to go professionally and personally. They are like a recipe or road map for success.

No matter what the industry, size, or state of your business may be, whether you are a brick-and-mortar generations-old family business or an entrepreneurial high-tech start-up that does business in the "cloud," conditions of satisfaction provide a foundation for driving change and a barometer for gauging how it's going. And I am stunned almost daily when I am talking to really smart leaders to see just how few of them can tell me what their personal conditions of satisfaction are. Even if you know what your company stands for—and that is a big if—you cannot lead it effectively if you don't know what *your* mission is.

I know my conditions of satisfaction in business: grow professionally, have fun, and make money. If I can't meet them working with or for a particular business, I don't go in. And when I am not meeting them over time, I get out.

Once you have established your personal conditions of satisfaction, you need to establish mutual conditions of satisfaction for change within your company. Businesses are change agents' customers, and conditions of satisfaction must link the two. You can't have conditions of satisfaction that are good for you but not for the business you are working with or for—even if you own it! What's good for me might not always be good for the business, and vice versa. The conditions of satisfaction might be similar, but they must also be mutual. That way, everything you try to achieve for yourself and your company is win-win.

Defining conditions of satisfaction and driving them through the company creates some tension (good) and stops a lot of wasted time on unnecessary projects and initiatives (even better). Think about all those open projects that never ended (or still have no end in sight). Most likely, people found out they didn't need them. They started when a department like Sales simply said, "I need this," or, "I *really* need that," but didn't sit down and define what the mutual conditions of satisfaction were for this and that. If they had done so, they might have found that they *really* needed something else. It's that sitting down and going through the mutual conditions of satisfaction that lets you find out what you and your people need.

So, what are your conditions of satisfaction? No, I'm serious. Stop reading now and write them down. Make them clear and concise. Everything else is just details. I'll be here when you get back.

Conditions of satisfaction are so important that any business can answer the following essential questions—questions that I cover in either this book or *The Mirror Test*—by returning to their conditions of satisfaction first:

- Do you really need to change, or do you just have a burr under your saddle?

- What kind of change do you need? Do you need a quick turn to avoid a collision, do you need a bigger course correction, or do you need to jump ship?

- Do you need new space or technology (hardware or software) if you are to compete?

- When do you know if you are making progress or if something is not working?

- What scares you the most? What is holding you back?

- What lifestyle do you want your business to provide?

- What does the end result look like?

Getting clarity in your own thought processes and confronting these questions is essential to selling the endgame to your people and yourself. And aligning your people and communities around the conditions of satisfaction is the foundation for success.

Let's consider the first question: do you really need to change, or is the problem just something irritating or annoying? Irritations like a dirty office and unprofessional-looking employees might be signs of larger problems affecting the mood of your business, a small issue you need to address in order to make things better, or just a bad day or week. So, ask yourself: "Are my conditions of satisfaction still being met, and is my breathing strong?"

If the answer is yes, your conditions of satisfaction just stopped you from tearing things apart in the name of action. The appeal of change is strongest when things feel stagnant or stuck—

but are they? You know what you are doing is right. The people and processes are working. Everyone is thinking big. Well, then, don't mess with it. Change for change's sake is bad. If you're bored, skip around or forward in this book and start thinking ahead, adapting your business, and anticipating your customers' needs. Find new and better ways to deliver on your brand promise and serve and communicate with your customers. Still bored? Find a hobby.

What about the next question: determining what kind of change you need? Conditions of satisfaction combat the feelings that can blind people and companies to the need to change or the reality that they need to get out. I've seen great companies, big and small—especially family businesses—go down because they got a little too comfortable clinging to what was. There's nothing wrong with being comfortable in business and in life, slowing down and appreciating what you have. I like doing nothing on Sunday, lying on the couch and watching a game, napping, and eating the crappiest food I can when my wife isn't looking. I like that. It's comfortable. But I had better be doing something on the other days to meet my conditions of satisfaction and hers.

How do you know when you are kidding yourself and you need to stop living in hope, saying things like, "Well, things are bad all over. At least I'm not as sick as the other guys"? Really? That makes you feel better? It makes me feel that you have forgotten your conditions of satisfaction and would fail the mirror test if you even bothered to take it. Get back to those conditions of satisfaction and remember why you're in the game in the first place. Look in the mirror and ask, "What is it that I want to get out of the business?" And if you can't see the answer, talk to other leaders or bring in a change agent from the outside who can look at things with fresh eyes and a different perspective.

The answers are not always cut and dried, but this process is a lot better than looking at only numbers and return on investment

(ROI) for answers. Now, ROI is an essential measurement tool that I see being used everywhere these days. And *overused*. Everything today seems to come back to ROI. Some things cannot be measured with numbers. You can try, but you will end up spending more time and money trying than you get out of the result.

For change agents, change is about making things better. Not everyone in a company is ready for that, but a change agent's job is to make the change as great as possible for the largest return, however that is measured:

- Sometimes it's measured in growth.

- Sometimes it's measured in margins.

- Sometimes it's measured in savings.

- Sometimes it's measured in customers.

- Sometimes it's measured in customer satisfaction.

- Sometimes it's measured in time.

- Sometimes it's measured in morale.

Your mutual conditions of satisfaction with your customer or your company can be as much about feelings as they are about finances. They are in the art of what you do. They help you push and stretch yourself to what you want to be and deliver on the promises you and your company make.

And when they are not being met, change or get out.

In 1932, George Eastman, who built Kodak into one of America's most powerful brands, made this point in one heck of a way. He asked his driver to take him around Rochester to see all that he had accomplished—not just Kodak, but the city and the universities to which he had donated millions. (Eastman's philanthropy put him in the same league as John D. Rockefeller and Andrew

Carnegie.) He then returned home and took his own life with a single gunshot wound to the heart. He was 77 years old. He had been in tremendous physical pain for years, but his suicide note did not mention this. It simply read:

"My work is done. Why wait?"

I prefer a less bloody but equally decisive exit strategy, but I can't imagine better words to explain what happens when my conditions of satisfaction are no longer being met. I've left businesses when I was making money because I wasn't having fun anymore or wasn't growing professionally. I admire people like Jerry Seinfeld and the team behind *Seinfeld*, Bill Gates, and countless other leaders who are far less well known who went out when they were on top for probably similar reasons. If business is good, but I find myself just going through the motions, not caring as much as I used to, I know I've peaked.

How do I know? I get back to my conditions of satisfaction. If I find that even though I'm still solving challenging problems or issues, the work isn't fun, I don't need to look at anything else in the business. Forget about the problems. Forget about ROI and marketing plans. I need a change. I need an exit strategy. My conditions of satisfaction are not being met. My work is done. Why wait?

Chapter 5

Principles mean something only when they are inconvenient. Prepare to live your brand promise in bad times and good.

We always want things to move *faster*, especially when we're changing, so it's tempting to take shortcuts and make compromises. In *The Mirror Test*, I talked about avoiding quick-fix "solutions" that are really Trojan horses (beware of Greeks bearing gifts), sales plans that generate buzz rather than revenue (remember: buzz is *not* sales), and big marketing and expansion plans that destroy your mood, strain your people, drain your resources, and have a negative impact on the quality of your products and services.

Much harder to challenge are the accepted ways of doing things in a company. Harder still is standing firm in your challenge when you feel uncomfortable, hate the way something is being done, or know that you *shouldn't* be doing that thing at all. It's easiest just to ignore these feelings and not act. Standing by your principles in these situations—when it is the risky and unpopular thing to do—is the test of a change agent's mettle. Remember: no one is going to die. You might get sacked, but your principles will ensure you land on your feet.

Let's start with the excuses. The fundamentals of change are always the same. So are the excuses for not changing: "We tried that before and it didn't work," and, "It's different here." No, you didn't, and no, it isn't.

I recently consulted for a company that had a product and process that really *was* unique. Its managers told me that billions of dollars, not to mention R&D complications and FDA regulations, were involved. Whatever—that's just more zeros and familiar problems on a larger scale. But when they told me that they were targeting their sales efforts at thousands upon thousands of people at pharmaceutical companies without having any idea of what those targets actually did at those companies? Whoa.

I'm all for a little ready, fire, aim, but this was not even ready. When I cut through the details and filtered the noise, what I discovered was that the process for marketing and selling this product was no different from what I had seen before. This company had spent tons of time and money on development, but it now wanted to speed through the sales and marketing process with an approach that was no better than throwing a bunch of darts at a dartboard and seeing what sticks. I stuck to my principles and made the company slow down and take the time to research the targets. This revealed that fewer than 100 people in the entire world made the decisions for the companies that needed this product, not thousands upon thousands. All those companies in the world and all those billions of dollars, and there were only 100 people that they needed to convince to transform their business. The company still needed to work hard to get to those people, but at least it had taken the time to get it right at the beginning.

Your employees must also be allowed to follow these same principles—to stop everything to do the right thing—without facing the risk of termination. When I was in the printing business, our company was having quality problems with the computers needed to run the printers. The computers needed to be configured differently for each printer brand, and we were consistently shipping computers with the wrong configuration in the name of speed. We were so driven to get the computers out on time that that was all we were doing: slapping on a label and thinking, "It may be wrong, but at least it's on time."

As soon as we discovered the problem, we held meetings, training sessions, and team-building exercises to address it. That's when we discovered that the people on the shipping floor knew this was happening, but said they didn't feel they could stop the process, even though they knew it was wrong. They were getting pressure from their bosses and their bosses' bosses to get the stuff out. They didn't agree with the decision, but they shipped the boxes anyway to get them out on time. Our CEO turned to the shipping manager and said, "You can stop that now. You can say no." He guaranteed that if the people on the shipping floor did this, they would not be fired, and as a result he empowered them and people at all levels in the company to change, stand by their principles, and do it right.

My biggest test of my principles came when I was at Kodak and we were launching this massive offset-class, knock-your-socks-off-with-its-quality-speed-reliability-and-price printer. Few of you will ever see printers like these. Basically, they look like gray boxes the size of semitrailers. You put trees in one side and thousands of pages a minute come flying out the other. They cost millions.

These printers were very important to Kodak, so we planned to launch them at a huge, important trade show. We reserved a stage and sent invitations for the press conference with the CEO and me.

And then I saw the printer and it looked like . . . a gray box the size of a semi. No.

Put simply, you can't be cool and look like Elmer Fudd—even if you *are* Elmer Fudd. And this was the Elmer Fudd of printers. I didn't want it to be something it wasn't. I just wanted it to be *the* Elmer Fudd of printers—*the* printer in its class. And it needed to look the part. We were telling people this product was amazing. We were saying it was the coolest, fastest, highest-quality printer of its kind *ever*. That image needed to be integrated into the printer. Our brand promise demanded it. We needed to be true to that promise. I went crazy.

"What happens when we pull back the curtain and it looks like this?" I told everyone involved in the launch. "I want people to be blown away. I want this to look like a Ferrari—like it's so fast it has fire coming out its ass."

Then I told them that if we couldn't do this, we would cancel the launch. People told me I could not be serious. But I was. This was not a game of chicken to see who blinked first. I was standing up for the brand. I was standing up for our principles, which were really inconvenient to stand up for at this moment—and expensive: my decision would cost money and time.

Now no decree—whether it be a new project or a change in something that's already planned—ever gets everyone aligned in agreement. There will always be people who think your way is the wrong way, even if they don't have another way. You can have input from some of those people some of the time. You can weigh some of their ideas and not others. But in the end, someone has to make a decision. In cases like this, that is usually left to the people who are least afraid of change. If I didn't say it, who would? And how would the people on my team know they could trust me to have their backs if they tried to stand for something like this down the road? Sure it was risky, but change agents can't hold back.

No one ever has to guess what a change agent is thinking. We tell you right up front. In this case, I put a stake in the ground to make an essential point: namely, that I was willing to stop this launch unless we could do it right. I knew we were going way beyond some people's limits. But I was doing what change agents do best: causing tension to push the brand.

And you know what? With no time to do it, the design team came back with a model with white on top and a red racing stripe down the middle. Better. And different. And probably as close as I was going to get to the Ferrari of printers. And in the days afterward, my team and the people who stood behind us started putting the backs of our hands on our butts and wiggling our fingers as we passed each other in the hall—our secret sign for fire coming out our asses and the empowerment that came with it.

Chapter 6

Change the mood, change the culture, then move on to people and processes. Remember: you can't be cool and look like Elmer Fudd!

I was riding the subway in New York City one afternoon when a sixtysomething gentleman sat down across from me. At first glance, he looked successful—nice tie, jacket, and slacks; a distinguished head of white hair. But then I began to process the details. Everything about this guy read success . . . *10 or 20 years ago.* Today his look read "better days behind me." His shirt and tie may have been expensive when he bought them, but now they were frayed and spotted. His pants and jacket were worn, if not threadbare, in places. He needed a haircut and a more careful shave.

Did I know this man? It doesn't matter. I made the same assessment of him that your employees, customers, and vendors make of you, your other employees, and your business every day. Sure, there could be any number of reasons for this guy's state. Maybe he was wearing his lucky outfit. Maybe he got into a rut long ago and stopped making that extra effort. Maybe his wife had died or could not see him literally coming apart at the seams. Maybe he thought he looked great and no one in his life had the heart to tell him the truth. None of these reasons matter to me. This is not personal, just as it is not personal to your people or your customers if your business looks and feels like this guy.

And don't start talking to me about "character." I love character. Not everywhere, of course. Pub: good. Hospital: no thank you—I want it to scream clean and healthy with lots of monitors and gadgets. Character is part of a pub's brand promise, not a hospital's, but if the staff and the water glasses at the pub looked and felt like the subway guy, I'd think twice about staying or ever coming back.

Don't start talking to me about "being comfortable," either. There is a big difference between dressing to be comfortable and looking like the human equivalent of peeling paint—a memory of something that had once been fresh and neat. As I said before, I like being comfortable, but it's easy to get so comfortable that you ignore the problems. It happens to all of us, but when it does, you need to deal with it, both when you start to change and then again when things are growing and going well, so you don't get too comfortable. Don't let a "that's the way it is" resign you to mediocrity and your business coffin.

And age has nothing to do with any of this; presentation does. No matter what your age, your business should look and feel alive. Mood is everything. That's why presentation is one of the key areas change agents attack first to transform a bad mood. Any business and its people can be changed to make a better presentation. In *The Mirror Test*, I talked about how I like to literally clean a business when I start working there or take it over, because presentation is both the easiest of those areas to change *and* the easiest to dismiss or ignore.

Too many businesses just don't care or can't or won't see presentation as important and take action to change it. Yet I can tell most of what's wrong with a business by walking around the place and sizing up the energy of its people. What does it feel like? Good or bad? Oppressive or productive? What are the people wearing? How do they handle themselves? When I walked around a gym I was working with, half the machines were out of order, the weights were a mess, and there were holes in the walls. The staff looked . . . wait . . . do you work here? Gyms are in the business of self-improvement, but nothing about the way this gym looked sent a message that anyone here cared about how I looked.

Put simply, bad mood can ruin a company faster than bad business. I hear leaders talk about changing the culture of a business, and I say fine, but the most important thing you can do is start by changing the mood. When you change the mood, you change the attitude and take the right steps toward changing the culture. Mood makes your place and your people feel that the business's best days are in front of it, and your conditions of satisfaction demand that.

You don't need a new space or all new stuff to have a good mood, either. I've been in businesses in buildings from the nineteenth century that felt new and exciting, with everybody hustling around, and I've been in businesses in brand-new office buildings that felt the exact opposite—their space and their people were just out of date. Start by doing what I do: walk around and make what construction people call a punch list: a list of things that need refreshing, repair, or replacement. Ask your people what sucks and recruit them to help fix it. The bad working conditions have affected them the most, so get them involved in the change. Enlist them as leaders in helping you create a new story for your business that everyone believes and has a stake in. Sure, some people can't do it. They resist. They can't help standing in your way. Now you can add those people to your punch list, too.

Some of you will read this and dismiss changes like these as cosmetic. But is beauty the only reason Oprah said women should change their hairstyle every two years? (Um, my wife told me that.) Can you really say clean clothes don't make you feel better? You stand differently. You look different. It doesn't matter whether the people in your business wear uniforms, come to work in jeans or business casual, or wear suits as long as the look is neat, fits the brand promise, and makes them feel good. This includes you—set the example. That's the reason I changed my jeans style and now wear custom-made skinny-butt jeans, which implies that I have a skinny butt, which if you know me, you *know* is not the case. But I digress . . .

The same thing is true in your business: if it looks disorganized and disheveled, it probably is. Remember: it can't be cool and look like Elmer Fudd! At the very least, addressing presentation companywide ensures that your people know you are paying attention. That's essential because the next step is to take a hard look at those people to get to the heart of most bad business: bad management.

Friendsourcing Mood

People who know me or have read *The Mirror Test* know that I love my family and my horses more than anything else in life and that my passion for change keeps me going in business. But what keeps me going day to day is Diet Mountain Dew.

So how happy do you think I am when my friend and sartorial master, Peter E. Roberti, president of retail sales at Adrian Jules Custom Clothiers, has a Diet Dew waiting for me whenever I come into the store? This is how mood can extend to more than just people and presentation—to your customers and thus to your bottom line. That's why Peter does this. And it's not just for me—he does this for all his customers, providing them with a great mood to match the company's great service. As Peter says, that is how the company competes: by making shopping an "experience—*the* experience of getting something custom made just for you. We've created an environment in our retail showroom, through the use of proper lighting, color, and décor that is inviting. We also offer gourmet candies, beverage service, and complimentary shoe shines to customers while they browse our finest selection of fabrics and the latest styles in men's fashions. Everything we do is centered on providing friendly personal service combined with prompt, dependable delivery of the finest custom-tailored garments available. It is never about price, but rather making sure that our clients are taken care of so that buying a custom wardrobe is a pleasant and rewarding experience."

When he was president of another advertising agency, John Favalo, now a managing partner at Eric Mower and Associates, recalls how he took my "cleaning" approach to cutting costs and thus got out of an economic downturn: "We needed to do something drastic to cut our costs and build morale, while our rainmakers danced. . . . We scoured the offices looking for waste of any kind, right down to pencils, pens, scratch pads, copy paper. We found lots of money sitting in drawers. Finally, we canceled all our office service contracts and split up cleaning, washing windows, and such among department leaders. One of my jobs was mopping the restroom floor. Soon everybody was helping. Any surpluses of any kind were pumped back into value delivery to clients or helping our rainmakers. We didn't just claw out of the recession, we slingshot out. And, in the process, we set high-water marks for teamwork."

And if your office is clean, then make sure the change you want to drive is also reflected in your internal materials—not just the ones you show your customers. Eben Swett, president and CEO of GISI Marketing Group, did this after he led a group that bought out the other shareholders by creating a document called "Values We Live By" that everyone from top to bottom would follow. Nice.

Be relentless in driving the change you want in your people and all parts of your business—be the change you want to see in the world.

Changing the mood in your business can lead to success. And if it doesn't, you will at least have fun as you go down! But you're sure to go down if you don't constantly and consistently drive the changes you seek throughout your business and empower your people to live and execute them in everything they do. Of course, changes are hardest to implement when you're dealing with deeply ingrained ways of doing business.

Two *years* before I joined Kodak as chief business development officer, the company had started reinventing itself as a digital company. It had spent millions to change its logo and imaging to reflect where it wanted to go. But when I walked into the lobby and through every hallway, dated, dingy pictures lined the walls. And I saw the old logo everywhere. It was on our letterhead, our e-mails, and most of our business cards. It was on our ID/security badges—the very things our people, their friends and family, and our visitors and customers and vendors saw us wearing every day.

The old logo was even on the top of our world headquarters. Here was an imaging company not walking its own talk.

Remember how I said I could tell 90 percent of what sucks in a company just by walking around and getting a feel of what is going on? Well, this sucked. The changes Kodak was making to its brand expectations and promises externally were not being driven throughout the company internally. What message were we sending to our people? Talk about a mood killer.

Of course, cost was the culprit. We had 14 years of letterhead inventory in storage; we needed to use up those cards; those identification and security badges cost a fortune; and don't even talk about the building signage . . . give me a break. If Kodak couldn't show we could do what we do for ourselves, how could we expect our customers to believe we could do it for them? Your branding goals should be as important as your financial and legal goals. You must consider the costs of *not* doing it (or in Kodak's case, the irony of an imaging company not changing its own internal image).

The rallying cry for change agents at this moment is, "Purge!" Leaders must purge this narrow mentality and clean the company from top to bottom. We need to put a proverbial stake in the ground and then act decisively. If we hit an obstacle, deal with it by removing it, going around it, or going through it. Keep fighting.

First I contemplated a bonfire to purge the paper problem, but that would have burned down a lovely building in the process, so I took a safer, more strategic approach: I put together a companywide presentation. What I wanted is what all change agents must want: to reenergize employees and make all of them brand champions. I detailed every change we needed. I explained how far we had come in our corporate transformation, but how we lacked focus internally. We were not engaging and empowering our people to reinforce our brand. We were not instilling brand awareness and loyalty. We did not believe in the change we were selling.

If we wanted employee excellence, pride, and passion, we needed not only to tell our people we wanted this, but also to show them we were serious. We needed to work together to create a shared "story" of what the company wanted to be, not where it had been.

I recruited a team to help. We started by taking down the paintings. We had the walls painted and hung new pictures. We hunted down every old envelope, letterhead, and label and recycled it. We created new branded print products and a standardized e-mail signature file with our new logo to present a consistent brand image.

We wiped out the old business cards. Actually, we went back to an old idea. Kodak's business cards used to be iconic: the first to have pictures on them. Now, new employees got photo-free cards with the old logo on them, while the senior employees never retook their photos and walked around with out-of date photos that looked like bad high school graduation pictures with ugly background colors. No. We updated the logo, restored individual employee photos on the front, *and* let the employees put their own photos on the back. My picture was me on my horse in South Dakota.

Yup, we allowed employees to personalize the back with their own photos—a personal branding statement that made our brand image their own, right there on their cards. You can imagine the hand-wringing and chaos that ensued over *that*. Legal and HR especially said we could not do it. "What happens if someone puts something inappropriate there?" I said I hoped someone *would* put something inappropriate there just to irritate everyone and lighten the place up. In the end, I added, "Don't you want to find the stupid people? That's how we'll find out who the stupid people are. Let them select themselves." That pretty much settled it.

Next, we got the lobby renovated *and* even got the sign on corporate headquarters changed. (And during the renovation, the team placed two business cards in the lobby cement: George Eastman's and mine. Cool.)

But that still left one thing: the ID badges. They were the most visible reminder of the old logo, and they turned out to be the biggest obstacle of all. Only new employees automatically got badges with the new logo and imaging. This punished the employees who had been there the longest and who most needed to be reminded of the company's changes. But badges were expensive to replace. I offered to pay for the changes, but Security and Legal still balked. This was *not* how they did things.

I didn't care. I told people to *just get them changed*. Then I did what any reasonable person would do: I threatened to cut them up.

I told everyone who worked at Kodak that if I saw anyone wearing an old name badge, I was going to cut it in half. I carried a pair of scissors to meetings and everywhere I went in the company so that people would know I was serious. And I was everywhere. When I was at Kodak, I ate in the cafeteria every day I could, not only because I liked the cafeteria, but also because it made me visible and kept me connected with everyone in the company, from top to bottom. The people whom I worked with and who worked for me had nowhere to hide.

People started "losing" their IDs, running over them, burning them with blowtorches . . . anything they could do to get new ones. The company noticed the increase in replacement badges, of course. And I heard some people had reported that I was going to cut up their badges if they did not change them. Rumor had it that I did it all the time. There were "witnesses"!

That's when I got the call to report to an internal inquisition at which a whole gaggle of obstructionists confronted me about my actions. It did not matter that I was a high-level officer in the company. They let me know it was inappropriate to cut up badges and that I did not have the authority to do so. I had to cease and desist. But they had bad intel.

"I'm not cutting up badges," I said.

"Oh, *really?* Come on, Jeff, we all know that you've done it. Everyone knows." They were muscling me, but I knew better.

"Everyone knows? Name me one employee. . . . Please give me the names. . . . You don't have them because it never happened. Have I *threatened* to cut up badges? Absolutely. Guilty as charged. What I did to them is no different from your threatening me now. Yes, I told them to lose their badges. I'm proud of the people who did. This is about our image to ourselves and our customers."

You have to have a big stick to swing and a whip to crack to create the tension you need—to get things moving and even start a change stampede. But you don't actually have to use them. I knew it was okay to act a little crazy. The people who line up against change agents are going to read us any way they want to, so why not push their perceptions and knock down some pins in the process? People only have to believe you would to believe in your top-to-bottom changes.

Around the same time, something really cool happened. Some of the employees who did not want to lie or rat me out (both things I respect) started making up nice labels with the new logo and placing them over the old logo on their badges. I never asked them to do this. The company and I had put them in a hard spot, but they believed in the change and found a way to make it happen. I swear I almost cried.

Every leader needs people like that. They were being problem solvers, creative and resourceful. They had become leaders and cheerleaders. They were all becoming my "clock changers" from the introduction—volunteering to run the gauntlet and surviving.

Chapter 8

Work across the seams of the company. Stick your nose into everything. Be a cheerleader *and* a white buffalo. Cause tension at every turn!

The gauntlet of change is cruel, and change agents are exposed to all of its dastardly personnel: naysayers, obstructionists, backstabbers, and opportunists who use the messiness of change to stand in the way or shoot down new ideas. People at Kodak (read: naysayers, obstructionists, backstabbers, and opportunists) liked to gossip about how I changed *everything* at Kodak—including, well, people.

Change agents know gossip is part of the gauntlet they must run, and Kodak was no exception. Firings that were part of layoffs that had been planned long before I became CMO? My fault. Obsolete divisions that were axed as part of the digital reinvention that had started before I was on board? My fault. And "they" certainly noted that my new teams in marketing proved I was changing *everything*. Only this time, they were right. But just as in the story about the badges, perception was not reality. You know how many new people I brought in at Kodak? One. I absolutely got rid of the wrong people and kept the winners. But then I looked at where the holes were skillwise and started to fill those holes by looking at the existing talent companywide, matching people's skills to the work required, and recruiting and hiring internally first. I knew that with the right leadership and direction, many people could help lead the change we wanted and were hungry for the chance! They just weren't empowered to lead or in the right positions to do so. Change agents must grant these people permission and cheer them on; remember: it takes a lot of strength to run this gauntlet.

In other words, get people in the right seats on the "bus," adapting the lesson on driving change that so many change agents learned from Jim Collins's still-outstanding *Good to Great*. Leaders are able to do this because they are seam operators—in effect, they operate across the seams of the company. We don't get involved in day-to-day processes outside of setting the operating principles. We don't need to know too many details; we've already been through a lot of this before, and we don't need it explained again. I tell my teams all the time, "I don't want to know or hear about how sausage is made unless someone died. I get it. It's sausage. Tell me what I need to know to get things moving."

What I want to find out is what is breaking down within the seams of my company—between people and groups and from process to process. That's what you listen to, and that's why listening is probably the best skill change agents can have—they listen throughout the organization and hear snippets from everyone and everywhere. That's how they find out what they don't know.

Change agents identify problems and then find ways to fix them or bring in people who can. This takes perseverance in a company of any size, even a small one, as the same excuses always pop up: "That's not my job. . . . That person or group does not report to me, so I have no authority. . . . That's not the way we do it. . . . That's not within my budget."

Change agents don't care about excuses or worry about offending the "authorities" when they are attacked. They can't. As with my approach to change at Kodak, they must act—and they must go on until someone tells them differently, and then deal with that obstacle. Here's why: the worst thing that happens is not that you make a mistake or piss someone off. Mistakes are inevitable, and it's our job to cause tension, which will occasionally piss people off. No, the worst thing is that you see something and don't bring it up—you become seduced by the process and become part of the problem by failing to change it.

Change agents are already facing a herd mentality. It's easier to blend in and go with the flow than to stand up and say, "Wait a second." Most animals survive by blending in with the herd. Who wants to be the white buffalo? That's the one the wolf targets.

Change agents are white buffaloes.

This is especially true internally. Making things happen requires change agents to live in those seams of the company, work across its silos, and stick our noses into everything. We cause tension as much as we cheer people on. We push as much as we praise. We are going to get more than our share of abuse from C-suite executives, managers, Legal, and HR, and also from those twentysomething employees with attitudes as big as buses and senses of entitlement to match who think—no, they *know*—they can do it better than you. Or how about that person who tells everyone how he heard "they" said you were awful to work for? And that person who ...

Sometimes you think you can fix the problem, sometimes you just see how hard the change is going to be, and sometimes you are just exhausted. Leaders cannot back down and must remember this lesson from the trail: "If you're ridin' ahead of the herd, take a look back every now and then to make sure it's still with ya." If you lose touch with the herd, things can turn bad fast, but if you are too close to the herd, you're eating dust. Whether you are leading thousands of people or just one, you need to find the right distance between the changes you seek within your company (employees, vendors, customers) and far enough ahead so you can actually *lead* them and not get caught up in how the sausage is made.

But your twentysomething employees with bad attitudes? There is something else you can do about them: fire them.

Chapter 9

You can teach a pig to kiss, but it usually gets messy and pisses off the pig. Please, please, please fire the right people.

Is it fair? Is it nice? Is it pretty? Is it the Christian thing to do? Who cares! Get rid of people who are not performing and trade up. The biggest effect on the day-to-day mood of your company is your people: identify the people who can't change, who are never going to change, or who don't believe that change is necessary to be successful, and *fire them.*

I'm not the first to say this. Perhaps most famously, Jack Welch fired the bottom 10 percent of his managers every single year and had a reputation for brutal candor with the rest. You need to make something like this happen in your company, too—and to make sure your people know it will happen. Be clear about your expectations, make sure they know the goals you want them to reach, let them make mistakes, document it all, and when it comes time . . . fire the ones who can't handle the ride.

Saying this, however, is the easy part. Actually firing people is the hard part.

And I'm just as bad at it as everyone else. No one *likes* to fire people. Even change agents who are new to companies and have no emotional connection to the people hate it—even *Donald Trump* sometimes feels terrible about using his catchphrase. It sucks. It's one thing if you're laying people off because of cutbacks, but firing people because you are changing and you have to tell them, "You're not meeting my expectations and doing what we asked you to do"? That's tough. But it's the right thing to do.

So how do you do it? The truth is, most leaders don't. They make a bunch of excuses for why they don't. They hem and haw over the costs of a search for new employees and retraining, as if this supposedly trained person is performing and isn't costing them in so many other ways. They think about the effect on unemployment insurance costs. They realize they failed to document performance and disciplinary problems and fret about the consequences or possible legal problems. (If you listened to me in *The Mirror Test* and wrote everything down, then you don't have this problem.)

The worst excuse is hoping people will change their behavior if we help them. We want to believe we can fix them. We hope for improvement and say maybe things are not as bad as they seem. This is the staffing equivalent of trying to turn a sow's ear into a silk purse. Remember the story of the scorpion and the frog? The scorpion asks the frog to carry him across the river on his back. The frog says, "No, you'll sting me, and I'll die." The scorpion says, "Of course I won't. If I sting you, we'll both die." The frog considers this and agrees, and the scorpion climbs on the frog's back. Halfway across the river, the scorpion stings the frog. "Why did you do that?" the frog asks. "Now we'll both die." The scorpion replies, "I can't help it. It's in my nature."

Sometimes we worry about how firing people will make us look and feel as a company. But turn the question around: How does your company look and feel with all these sow's ears? What are they doing to the mood of the place and the people you want to keep? In the end, I have never felt I made a mistake in firing someone. Usually, I think I should have done it sooner.

How bad can this problem get? A business I worked with as part of a TV show pilot had an employee who was stealing from it, only the owners didn't tell me that. It came up only when the producers noticed rules for how to conduct a polygraph exam and employee rights when taking a polygraph test hanging on the wall. That's not something you usually see on the wall of most businesses. In this case, the employee (a friend of the family—oh, boy, here come the excuses) had failed a polygraph five times. *Five* times. Huh? Even if this weren't the case—even if the managers just felt the employee was dishonest and was stealing from them— why would they want that employee around?

Stop thinking about the why nots and *act*. Should you discuss the problems first? Sure. It honors good employees to have those kinds of conversations. *Maybe* you can move past the problems with the best people. Maybe you can set new levels of expectations. Examine why the employee is resisting your changes. Is it grounded in deep principles? Typically it is not. Most of these people are not living up to their full potential, but instead are preventing change by fighting to protect the way things used to be. They need to go now.

But if what the employee is doing *is* principled? Well, that is not a bad person to have on your team to add perspective. For example, employees who are willing to speak up in any situation can be useful in expressing concerns or seeing potential that you don't—as long as they will be willing to kill for whatever decision you make and not try to kill *you*. But usually? They are just scorpions, and they need to be confronted before they align people against you or even influence them. Don't play games. Don't give them the satisfaction of knowing that they are getting to you, and stay ahead of them. You know if you get the momentum going, they can't stop it. Identify them and get them in the right place or get them out.

Think you need to be clearer about what the conditions of satisfaction are before you act? Bring everyone together and say, "This is where we're going." I don't care if you have 8,000 people or 8, if they are outsourced or in-house, or if you have millions on the line or thousands. Make clear what the expectations are. Let everyone know that some of them can make the journey and others can't. That will help you find the kind of people you want and change the rest out. It's always easier to change the person in the job than to try and change a person.

Not sure whom to get rid of? Ask your best employees. You've probably fired someone in the past and had another employee come up to you and say, "Yeah, he was a problem," or, "I'm so glad you did that." Employees know, and they will feel empowered as long as you ask them honestly and do not make them feel like tattletales.

Yes, sometimes you can't make wholesale staffing changes because it will strain and hurt the company, while other times you need to cut quickly. Firing people is a balancing act. But no one's going to die when you do it.

Besides, do you really think most people don't know it is coming? Some of them may not, but most do. Heck, they might even be better off afterward. They need a push out the door and into something that's better for everyone. Most will leave calmly, if sadly, but some will be vicious. (One person I fired changed all my passwords and my frequent flyer number and then rerouted some of my flights.)

Firing people doesn't mean you think they're not wonderful people. Maybe you want to have them over for dinner or grab a drink. But still fire them. Tell them you love them and you'll miss them, but you're letting them go because you have conditions of satisfaction, and they're not cut out for what you need. And remember: fire yourself from the jobs you're not good at, too. No good at details? Stop doing the books! Not good with people? Bring in someone who can smooth things over for you.

One time, a staffer of mine ran into a former employee who she said now had a terrific job and was very happy. She also told me, when asked what he thought of the company and me, that he fairly glowed.

"Oh, really?" I said. "That's interesting, because I fired him."

I was not surprised he had a good job, and maybe I shouldn't have been surprised about the kind words, either. That guy had a great attitude and a great personality, but he just couldn't live up to my expectations. My job was not the right job for him.

Friendsourcing Whiners and Dopes and Skunks—Oh My!

There's an old saying in the business world that being in business would be great if it weren't for all the customers and employees. And let's face it: most of your mood issues come down to your people, or, as my pal Miles Young, chief executive officer at Ogilvy & Mather Worldwide, put it, "Whenever I see anything that sucks in the business, the first thing I do is to look at the people around that thing. Things don't break by themselves; they get broken as a result of negligence or mistakes—and so often these go back to people. In many cases, we need to change people."

Damn right. Why do we pay so much attention to these people and give the floor to the complainers when the quiet, high-quality majority is saying, "Shut that guy up!" This is why I nodded in absolute agreement with Willis Turner, president and CEO at Sales & Marketing Executives International, Inc., when he said that the number one thing he's done wrong in the past is "hold the hands of whiners. Whiners just plain suck all the energy up and give nothing back." Or why I laughed when John Favalo, managing partner at Eric Mower and Associates, told it like it is when he revealed he would do everything in his power "to elevate the hiring process and prevent hiring dopes. Dopes suck the life out of a business. They cause mistakes, reverse productivity, impact morale, and—in the worst case—lose you business. The right kinds of people are the suckage stoppers who fill up your business with the stuff it takes to succeed."

Nice. You can move only as fast as your lowest common denominator, so fire the whiners and look for winners. Dump the dopes. But don't stop at getting rid of the dopey, whining people: stop thinking about them and forget about them when they are gone. This includes anyone who acts like what Pete Deutschman, chief buddy at the Buddy Group, called a skunk. Pete learned this the hard way when a client stiffed his company and stole its code: "We did everything our lawyers told us to do, but the loss of revenue and ongoing attention to legal put a strain on our cash flow, and we had to settle just to make payroll. We switched our focus from fighting on what is owed to fighting for what we love, and that is doing good work for our clients. By appreciating the good clients we have and not focusing on the one skunk . . . we prevailed and are 100 times stronger as a result." Oh, those skunks. I slap myself for doing the same thing.

Finally, while you're at it, make sure your policies and procedures don't tilt toward ways of dealing with all these whiners, dopes, and skunks. Why design around the negative as if all the positive people would or could do the kinds of things the whiners and the dopes always do. You can't rule-make your way to good behavior. Yes, protect yourself from problems, but let's not prioritize those people who take you down the wrong Yellow Brick Road, so to speak. Be bigger than that. Most people display good behavior, so as Jim Meisenheimer, president of Jim Meisenheimer, Inc., said, it is better to avoid making these big mistakes: "Hiring fast and firing slow, providing your top per-formers with underwhelming recognition, and being a poor role model for your employees." And remember, all your poor per-formers, not to mention the whiners, dopes, and skunks, also prevent you from scaling your business up and down. As my friend Paul Edwards, president of FormStore Incorporated, told me, "Businesses must be scalable. Look at sales revenues, look at processes, look at staffing, and then cut the deadwood from the tree. Then cut again. Even a healthy tree must be pruned to thrive. Are employees contributing to company profits in a way that makes them promotable in your organization? If not, they are blocking the ladder and preventing your company and your employees from growing."

Chapter 10

Great people, like great
horses, don't want to
get in the trailer
even if they know they
are leaving a bad place.
Make them want to go.

Unless you are truly unique, the *only* difference in most industries between you and your competitors is your people. When I owned my printing company, I owned the same equipment as other printers. I had the same software and paper stock. My customers might say that how we delivered our results, our service, and the way we operated was a distinction, but it was my people who determined the quality of those things.

The only thing that set my company apart, aside from the way we looked, was my people—the relationships they built and what they did for me. My best people worked hard to find ways to do it cheaper, faster, greener, with less money or people—whatever I needed. And when it comes to your customers and vendors, they are going to see your people more than they see you. They have to like the service that they get from them, not just your company.

That's why change agents work hard to help their best people. Because when you're changing, even the best people can be difficult. Think about my horse, Glue, from the introduction. Glue's a good horse, even though he makes things difficult. But is he my best horse? No, Blaze is. Blaze is magnificent. And yet he can be just as difficult as Glue when it comes to getting into the trailer. Does that make him a bad horse? No. Difficult, sure, but I would rather have a stable of racehorses that are difficult and hard to handle than a group of nags who are colicky and whiny.

Blaze, like the best employees that I want on my change agent "ride," just needs help getting where I need him to go. So how do I get my Blaze-like employees to embrace change? The same way I get Blaze to: make them want to go there.

First of all, asking Blaze to get into a confined, unnatural space is against his whole instinct. I mean, how do you think horses have survived for thousands of years? They flee from any potential danger or, if they are my horses, work! That's why you never look horses in the eye: they think you are going to kill them. Look them in the eye as you approach them in the pasture and they'll immediately walk away from you or flee. You need to bring them in gradually. So imagine what it's like when they have to get into that trailer. Ain't no amount of pushing and pulling (force) that'll make it happen. Maybe you try a bucket of oats or other rewards. But they know. They're not stupid. They'll figure out that the reward is actually a trick to get them to do something they don't want to do rather than what it should be: a reward for doing something well. They know you're gonna bind them down and take them somewhere that they don't instinctively want to go.

So ditch the oats and do what I do with Blaze, which is the same thing I did with Glue: make it uncomfortable for him not to do what I want. I walk him up to the trailer and say how great it will be if he gets in. Then I pull him away and run him around in circles, twitching him lightly to get him agitated, so he does not like it. Then I walk him up and make it calm. After three or four times, that horse will run into the trailer.

That's what leaders must do with their people: make everyone uncomfortable where they are so everyone *wants* to move forward. Employees often have the same instinct when facing changes: resist the changes and keep doing what they want to do or flee (quit). Their tendency is to go back or to avoid the conflict, and this leads to a herd mentality in the wrong direction.

So how do you stop that? Well, first make sure your people understand where they are going and how they are getting there. The familiar analogy of a bus is probably better than a trailer here, so tell them why getting on the bus is different and great—not *easy*, but great. Then, if they continue to prefer the old ways of doing things, call them out on it and praise them when they do the things that are right. Make sure there are no rewards for bad behavior. If they get a good result but do it the old way, thank them, but do not praise them, and explain to them why you did not. And make sure they know that the bad behavior has consequences— from poor evaluations to getting fired.

This is not about helping one person—focusing your energy on one person can cost you the team and the mood you worked so hard to change. Your job as a change agent is to get people to feel the same way and work together. And this is incredibly hard to do. So do what the Vikings did: make it impossible to do anything else.

The Vikings were powerful explorers. They landed on shores prepared to conquer. But when they arrived, those shores were sometimes filled with a lot of other people who had arrows and weapons. Maybe they were not as good as the Vikings' arrows and weapons, but they were still pretty accurate. It could give a junior Viking pause. So to convince the landing team to move forward together and never look back, they burned the boats. Without the boats, there *was* no way to go back.

Convince your team the same way. The reason I changed from the horse analogy to the Vikings here is that part of the horse analogy does not work: you *must* look people in the eye when you talk to them. Never lie. Never say that the battle to change things will be easy. It won't be. That's a surefire way of getting even the best people to flee before you even set sail. If you do that, you may find no one is with you when you get there. Instead, be honest and transparent about what you want to do and where you are going. Tell your team members that everybody has weapons, so there will be a fight, but this is the only path to growth. Tell them to think big so the company can grow bigger with them.

And remember: when you're going through a lot of change, fatigue can set in. Think of your best people as leaders whom you push to be better and smarter. Keep being their biggest cheerleader as you do it, too. This is one of the most important jobs a change agent has. Leaders have to know their people will have their backs, and to achieve that, you've got to win them over and get them to commit to coming along. And to get them there, you might need to cause some tension, too, to convince them you know the best way forward. So, burn those proverbial boats so no one, including you, can go back. Even if it costs you a battle or a war, when you get there, burn the boats.

Friendsourcing Inspiration

When I asked my friends, "Where do you get your inspiration for change?" I got the answers I expected: books, magazines and newspapers, trade shows and journals, speeches, leaders in industry (theirs and beyond), other change agents, artists, customers, their children, coffee, Red Bull, Diet Mountain Dew—whatever. They all agreed that driving change is exciting and just out-organizing and out-hustling the competition is inspiring. But what source of inspiration excited the change agents I surveyed more than any other? Their people—the fact that every person on their teams and any new people they hired had the opportunity to drive change. So, change agents have to do several things when it comes to people.

Find Them

Pay more money for people who bring you solutions rather than whining about the problems. As Miles S. Nadal, chairman, founder, and CEO of MDC Partners, Inc., says, "Smart people drive business transformation. Empower them to do so. These individuals will ensure your organization is influential and nimble enough to innovate—to enable progress rather than avoid it."

Make Sure You Find Them on Every Level

Don't spend so damn much time on the managers and executives that you forget the frontline people. Russ Mann, CEO at Covario, speaks for the many change agents who responded that "not just the executives, but even young new frontline people bursting with ideas and innovation—every new person—has the opportunity to drive change—both positive and negative. Adding new people drives change more than anything else."

Make Sure They Have What Is Needed for the Situations They Will Face

As Sarah Fay, an independent board advisor in the emerging media space and the former CEO of Aegis Media North America, said, "We needed to have a culture of change—people who could deal with a shifting landscape; people who could deal with ambiguity; people who were resilient to being told no; people who just believed there was value in the proposition of digital marketing." Or as my South Dakota pal Dr. Tracy J. Smith, co-owner of Natural Arts Chiropractic & Acupuncture, said: "I can teach someone how to run our software, file paperwork, or transfer a phone call, but I can't teach someone how to genuinely smile and brighten the day of a patient who didn't sleep all night due to back spasms."

Train Them

As Jeff Cleary, owner and managing director of Catalyst, told me: "When restructuring the entire agency from the ground up, we missed the cultural challenges of change. We woefully overestimated our organization's ability to adapt to change. It cost us a year of revenue growth and caused an enormous dip in morale. If I had a do-over, I would have stayed more personally involved from the get-go and provided more hands-on training. I would have involved my staff more in the implementation of the change and boosted their comfort level with their new job functions."

Actively Manage Them

As Miles Nadel also noted, "We take on the crucial task of managing investments of human capital—namely, talent—to build the strengths and capabilities of our partner network. Our now disciplined focus on talent as the single greatest business advantage has driven the evolution and transformation of MDC Partners, and has driven measurable return on investment for our shareholders. We have never looked back."

Retain Them

As Ronn Torossian, CEO of 5W Public Relations, says about building one of the top 25 U.S. public relations firms (in an industry famous for its turnover), "Realize just how hard it is to find and retain really good, strong people. Growing (and retaining) my nearly 100 employees is more important than any individual action I can take."

Chapter 11

Accept and encourage mistakes! Mistakes help you assess your team and determine if you need to recruit people or skilled technicians.

Xerox was formed when Kodak rejected its idea for a new kind of copier. Apple was founded when Xerox rejected Steve Jobs's idea for a new personal computer. John Travolta could have been Forrest Gump; Tom Selleck passed on being Indiana Jones; Gwenyth Paltrow told James Cameron that *Titanic* was not her "cup of tea." People love tidbits like these and imagining "what if." But do these companies and actors do that? Do they call their decisions mistakes? Do you? Whatever you or they call them, the point is these companies and actors did not let these decisions define what and who they are. They know you can't change what's behind you, only what is in front of you.

Unfortunately, too many leaders and companies do the opposite when mistakes are made. They dwell on "what if we had done this" rather than "what if we do this," which is the very foundation of change.

Change agents know they can always lose, but, win or lose, mistakes will be made. We're gonna screw up! No matter how prepared you are and how good your team is, a lot of bad (and good) luck will be undeserved. Learn to get over it now. Mistakes are inevitable. Of course you should try to minimize them. But just as you must realistically evaluate your business given current market conditions and the need and possibilities for change, you must be realistic and accept that mistakes will happen.

One year at the Consumer Electronics Show in Las Vegas (the biggest show of the year), our team at Kodak tried to push the brand to feel cooler and hipper by cutting a deal with three young women with established blogs to interview us and blog about our brand. Good move; good self-started initiative. They posted their videos, and we posted links to those videos on our website and blog and then publicized them to all our employees and community. Great! Except that below one of those videos posted on their site was an ad for another site that talked about the 10 best places to see something offensive in Las Vegas. As you can imagine, that got back to our employees at Kodak, and I got a phone message from the chief diversity officer asking why we had done this and had I known what was going on. Of course I hadn't. I don't filter my team or censor our partners' ads. I simply talked to the team members, determined they had been unaware of it too, and decided we should just not promote that video link on our site. Easy solution to sustain our team's initiative.

That's your first lesson in accepting mistakes: don't let the perfect get in the way of the good—you're not perfect, so don't believe that anyone else can or has to be. In fact, in this imperfect world, no mistake will cost you unless it is unacknowledged and uncorrected or un-encouraged.

Yes, I said *un*-encouraged. I believe that if you have the right people in the right positions, mistakes will mostly be of two types:

- *Inescapable errors.* Acknowledge and correct them to create awareness and team play. They are useful early in the change process in finding out whether you have a team that is responsible and accountable and capable of driving the change you need. Can you get ahead with the team you have? What are its weaknesses?

- *Missteps that come from thinking big and trying to grow bigger.* Acknowledge and encourage them; they indicate a willingness to go for opportunities and not play it safe, refusing to resign oneself to mediocrity. Who wants bland? Go for it! Do you need more people or skilled technicians to help you do this?

Look at the mistakes your team members make and how they handle them to answer questions and to help you assess what your team can do and where you need new blood.

Any quarterback or coach knows it's okay to miss a block. What happens next is most important. Say I'm the quarterback and the team is huddling up after Tyler missed a block that cost us some serious progress on the drive. First of all, I expect Tyler to be the first one to acknowledge to the team (not just to me) that he screwed up—I expect Tyler to hold himself accountable, and *so should Tyler.* Don't shake your head and let the mistake define your perception of Tyler. And don't let the rest of the team get on Tyler's case either and talk trash about a teammate. Accept it and correct it together.

Most of the time players like Tyler bounce back. But what happens if Tyler doesn't bounce back? What if your corrections fail and this is not a one-time or one-game screw-up, but instead he keeps missing blocks throughout the game and all season long? Of course, you replace him with someone who plays the same position—either someone who's already on the team or at the company, or someone from the outside. Move him to another position or move him out.

What's more interesting is when Tyler comes back to the "huddle" or you talk to him after the "game" and he says something like, "Usually I can handle the competition, but now they are twice as big and fast. I need some help out there." Change agents have great respect for that. He's holding himself responsible and accountable and being very aware of his limitations in the face of the competition. He's reporting from the front lines that things have changed, and while he could handle the competition before, he can't handle it now, or at least not alone. You need to find a way to get him help or find another person to put out there who is just as fast and powerful. Find a way to keep using those people by pairing them with the new people and skilled technicians you bring in!

When you are turning it on change-wise, you *want* but cannot *expect* all your people to rise up with you. Look at my own operation: I'm constantly talking to my team members about thinking big and acting bigger. But they get bogged down in details. They'll come to me and say, "Jeff, we shouldn't do that; it costs thousands of dollars." Well, who asked you to tell me how much it costs? I asked them to get to another level with me and to think at that level, not be limited. I did not tell them there was a budget. Sure I want to be frugal. I want people like that in my finance operations, not on my execution team. I want them to achieve greatness with lots of zeros on the end. And the best way to do that is to swing and swing hard, not bunt safely. That's thinking small, and I now know I need new people to think big.

Some companies have come up with clever ways to transcend these problems, like making other people think big for them. When Netflix couldn't create a new algorithm that increased the accuracy of what kind of movies people would like based on previous rentals by 10 percent, it offered $1 million to anyone who could. (The prize was claimed in 2009 by an international team of seven people.) Later, as you grow bigger, we'll see how you can enlist your customers to help you do this, too. (Don't necessarily look to Netflix for more examples without a big prize attached, though. The company's move to change its pricing structure—a move it really had no choice but to make—caused huge customer blowback, both to the hike *and* to the way it was communicated to its customers, undoing much of the positive perception of Netflix.)

Some companies buy their way in through acquisition. Kodak couldn't transform its existing business into a digital brand, so it bought several companies that could. But even if you buy your way into competitiveness, you need people to run those businesses. That's why companies like Facebook often acquire a business solely to get the people. For example, it bought Bret Taylor's FriendFeed for cash and stock, and Taylor soon became Facebook's chief technology officer. "We have never once bought a company for the company," Facebook founder Mark Zuckerberg said at Stanford's 2010 Startup School. "We buy companies for excellent people." That's what you can do when you have Mark Zuckerberg's billions.

Most companies don't have that kind of cash in their pockets, but even if they did, it wouldn't make a lick of difference if those people can't function as a team or if they can't make your people function that way. That's why you must work hard to always, always be recruiting people who are like you, even if you don't have the business to hire them yet. Start by quietly finding out who the best people are, both inside your company and outside it, at your competitors. (Another reason to shop your competition.) Who impressed you with the results she got for a competitor? Who shares your spirit? Who's following you on social media sites? Whom are you following? Whom do you meet at industry events, conferences, mixers, appearances, parties, and so on? Whom do you read about in trade and other media? Who impresses you?

Start now. Make a list of freelancers and salaried employees at other companies—even if you can't or don't want to approach them yet and tip your proverbial hand. At least know who they are. The speed of change mustn't be slowed by unnecessarily long-drawn-out searches.

Friendsourcing Fear of Failure

When I asked my friend Linda Sawyer, North American CEO of Deutsch Inc., how she inspires her team to change, she said, "The most effective way to spread and fuel inspiration with your team is by making everyone feel that part of their job description is being a change agent." I love that. Then, Linda added that what helps her team members drive that change is her allowing them to "be fearless and not afraid of failure. If you don't take risks, experiment, or empower people to put themselves on the line, you will never innovate, advance, or evolve." I love that even more.

Every one of your people should have this mentality. Don't you want that? Being fearful gets in the way of success and taking those chances. Or as Miles Young, chief executive officer at Ogilvy & Mather Worldwide, said to me, "Fear of failure is the single most creative force in business. The difficulty, though, is being fearful. People—and business owners in particular—develop layers of complacent insulation, self-justification, and pain avoidance, which come as an unfortunate concomitant of just surviving in their jobs."

Richard Lobel, executive vice president at CBS Radio Altitude Group and CBS RIOT, and John Favalo, managing partner at Eric Mower and Associates, also commented on complacency and putting up with the status quo as death knells for change agents. Richard said, "I fear becoming complacent and giving in to 'well, that's the way it is always done.' I don't want to become a creature of habit that results in creating artificially imposed constraints on decisions and ideas simply because it is easier."

John used almost the exact same words when he told me about, "The six dirty words: we've always done it that way. I see it in our clients and in us. Breakthrough is often the reward for risk. If you always do the same thing, the same way, will you break through? I don't believe so. Nor do I believe you will challenge your people to be the creative dynamos they can be."

In business, there's nothing wrong with mistakes. Sure, failure is not an option if you are Gene Kranz, the flight director of the failed *Apollo 13* mission to the moon, and you have only a few hours to get your astronauts home safe. (Kranz's autobiography is called *Failure Is Not an Option*, although he never uttered that line; it was written for his character in the Ron Howard movie *Apollo 13*.) But you're not Kranz: no one is going to die! Failure can actually drive your team to success if its members are unafraid of the consequences of acting fearlessly. As Joe Abruzzese, president of sales and marketing for Discovery Communications, said, "What drives successful change is the removal of the consequences of failure during the change process. Even if the change fails to deliver results, the act of change should be applauded and supported at the top of an organization. When I was made head of sales at CBS, my boss said to me, 'I want you to change the way we represent ourselves to the ad community. Just don't do it like your predecessor and I'll be happy.' That inspired me to move forward. In one month, we totally restructured the sales department; 90 percent of the people had new roles, a new look. They were challenged and had an opportunity to take a fresh look at their new roles. Most of the staff embraced change, and they prospered. Some stuck by the old methods and eventually left the company."

In other words, don't let your people act out of fear and hold back that little extra, and don't you do it either. If they can't do it when you're changing and encouraging them to think big, they never, ever will.

Chapter 12

Got people in the right positions? Great! Now ensure respect for each position, and then get the heck out of the way so you can lead.

Once again, success comes down to the one difference between you and your competitors: people (including you). So while it is one thing to get people in the right positions, making sure they know how to *play* those positions is equally if not more important.

A football team is responsible for executing plays that require a complex set of movements with multiple options that need to be deployed depending on what happens during the play and what the competition does and throws at you. If your team fails to play its positions and loses sight of the short-term goal of the play and the long-term planning for both the drive and the game itself, things can fall apart fast. Not only will you lose the game, but you're likely to get knocked out, which in business, as in football, means not just that your team will lose, but that its members will lose faith in you and align themselves against you.

To stop this, quarterbacks huddle their teams during drives to make quick adjustments and ensure everyone is clear on what just happened and what comes next. You huddle, listen, clap your hands together as a team, and say go. (No-huddle offenses are used only when speed is essential and require even more planning and precision in their execution by their quarterbacks. You need to learn to huddle first before you can reach this level of play.) That's what you must do with your team to make sure it is "still with ya" and that everyone knows his position and his value to the team.

Imagine if everyone huddled and said, "Throw me the ball! I'm open!" No! It's great that people want the ball (and between "games," you should see if they can handle it), but people have to play their positions. After all, not everyone can have the ball. If everyone is wide open, it's because they're *not supposed* to be open. They should be someplace else. The play—and the team—is likely to fail if people do not do the jobs they were assigned.

In business, I see this happen with service agencies that try to do more than just create the work they've been hired to do. They want all your business, and that's understandable. They need to grow, and that's understandable, too. But while bigger is better in theory, it is not better in this case, especially if it detracts from the work you do well. One size does not fit all. Yes, you should make sure your customers know you offer additional services, and you should develop new services and talent as you adapt (as we shall see later), but deliver on your core promises first. Doing otherwise will confuse your customers and distract you from the tasks at hand.

Small, focused, and specialized can be best and lead to great results to build on. *Small is bad only if you're not thinking big!* I once was going to set up an international World Trade Center franchise in Sioux Falls before I realized that my state's vision of import/export was limited to Iowa. That's not thinking big to act bigger.

Remember: a brand is nothing more than a promise delivered, and delivering great results on the promises you have made
comes down to team performance, not size or individual position. High-performance teams know this. They anticipate what's
going to happen together. They have players in all the right positions who understand the value and the service they provide.
They trust one another. They expect to win regardless of who or
what they face. They deliver.

And they *respect* one another regardless of their positions.
I learned the importance of this as an all-state football center. I
snapped the ball to the sexiest position on the field and then never
saw it again. But I knew my job and performed it well, and my
team respected me. In turn, I learned to have respect for other
people who could help me do my job. For example, as center, I
liked to have the ball laid in a certain way with the laces up when
we broke the huddle. And I got it by asking the ref to do it for
me. In return, I called him sir and found the ball and handed it
to him after the play whenever I could. That's how I learned to
treat anyone who helped me have a great day with respect, too—
everywhere: vendors, waiters and waitresses, truck drivers and
delivery people, mailroom workers. When they know you're
watching and you value what they do, they work harder, improve
the mood, and help you succeed.

And don't let your people disrespect each other by triangulating, either. Here's how that goes: Jim and Jeff don't like each
other and don't get along. Jeff is sick of it and starts to draw Sue
into their problems, complaining about Jim at every opportunity.
Sue now starts altering her opinion of Jim because of the bad stuff
she's hearing from Jeff, and she starts having problems with Jim.
That's triangulation: three people making up the points of a tri-
angle with only two points talking. Whether the accusations are
true or not, leaders need to stop the triangulating as soon as they
become aware of it. When Sue comes to you, start by asking her if

she has talked to Jim, and if she hasn't done this yet, either make her do so or get all three of them in the room and talk together.

As you can see, communication is key to attacking all of this, but so is getting out of your head. When an employee takes an unusually long lunch, what's your first instinct: interviewing at another company? Do you ask yourself if that employee *really* sounded sick when she called—even the one who is rarely sick and has never showed you anything but loyalty? Do you think everyone in your office is looking for a way to put one over on you? Don't give in to paranoia and believe the bad stuff about employees with no foundation. Don't assume they are all looking to put one over on you. At the very least, look for patterns, and even if you find them, make sure the patterns really are what they seem to be.

I remember when I had come to believe that one of my people was always going to be late with something because, quite frankly, she always was. She did great work, but she continually had an excuse—her father was in the hospital, she had an e-mail problem that couldn't seem to be solved, and so on. And when a client complained about her, I looked through the client's glasses and knew I needed to replace her.

But I was looking through the client's eyes, not mine. I needed to step back, move past my personal opinions, and resist believing the bad stuff first. I asked myself, "How am I viewing this?" If you can't do this, call someone who can—not to complain about the person and reaffirm the negative, but to see what you are not seeing before you respond with hellfire. In this case, I stepped back and found out that all the things she had said were true. Her father was very sick. Her e-mail was completely screwy. By responding positively, I could help her overcome those obstacles and continue to do great work.

All of this you learn to do by playing quarterback as a change agent. You huddle with the team. You see from the proverbial trenches how things are working, and your team members know that you understand what it takes. After all, every quarterback must throw a block now and then. Nothing can be beneath you. That's why, when I ordered my team to clean the businesses I bought, I was also there with a bucket getting dirty.

Yet just as I can't keep cleaning the floors, leaders can't stay at quarterback or they will lose the big picture and fail to deliver on their conditions of satisfaction and the mutual conditions of satisfaction they have developed with the company they work for. Eventually, they must make the transition from leading in the huddle to coaching and leading the whole team, thinking ahead about plays—even games—and answering to their bosses. (Coaches answer to owners just as CMOs answer to CEOs; CEOs answer to shareholders, investors, partners, and the market; and all of them answer to customers . . . someone is always your boss.)

So get people in the right positions and then step away and out of the day-to-day mess of the huddle. Stay in touch, but let your leaders lead and get out of their way.

Friendsourcing Getting Out of Your Way

It's one thing to learn to fire yourself from the jobs you aren't good at; it's another thing to learn to fire yourself from the jobs you are good at but shouldn't be doing. There are things in business I can do and do well, but I choose not to do. I might do them efficiently and take great pride in doing them, but I can't waste my time, because time is the only thing I can't get more of. Hire people to do those jobs and fire yourself. My agent, Wendy Keller of Keller Media, Inc., always tells this to her authors. All of them are people who can market, so few of them take her marketing advice for their books: "Sometimes they try to reinvent the wheel or do their own thing or hire the wrong (or dumb) people to support them, which rarely works." In other words, they can't get out of their own way.

Remember: time is the one commodity that everyone has in equal amounts. Does your schedule reflect the priorities you are trying to drive? I always say you can do anything I can do in marketing, promotion, business development, and PR given money, time, and expertise. The only variables are the expertise and the money. You can work more hours, of course, but what time really comes down to is choices and deciding what you can and will pursue to the best of your ability. And as Wendy told me, this goes for your personal life, too. In fact, she wishes she had taken this advice on the *most* personal and culturally loaded level for a woman: as a parent. Yes, with her daughter: "The number one thing I should have done differently, the biggest thing that would have changed the way my professional life unfolded, is this: hire a nanny when my daughter was in elementary school. Women are infused with massive guilt over their parenting choices, no matter what they are. Had I relinquished the 3 to 6 p.m. slot to someone else, I would have been a better manager to my employees, a much less frazzled professional, a more relaxed single parent, and probably a better mom."

I think it's pretty brave of Wendy to admit she feels this way—that she did not have the time to do both these things and as a result probably fell short on both at times. I'll remember what she said when I think about the little things I *shouldn't* be doing (like clearing the snow from the driveway) and eliminate the things that get in the way of winning in business *and* in life.

Chapter 13

Be direct and talk about the elephants in the room. Even ride 'em and teach 'em tricks—it's a better way, even if it feels wrong.

One of my favorite business cartoons shows a man presenting a chart on which the line graphing his project's progress starts in the middle, climbs a bit, and then falls dramatically. The caption is a question from one of the men being presented to: "Would you please elaborate on 'then something bad happened'?"

I used this slide in presentations about Kodak to illustrate the decline of film and the company's need to adapt and become a digital company or die like RCA, Oldsmobile, Polaroid, and other great American brands. But the cartoon is equally good for illustrating the importance of talking about elephants in the room. I know, because something similar happened to me in one of my "elephant moments."

I was not a CMO at my company, but I had been asked to join the CMOs and top people from Sales and Marketing in a meeting about the dot-com side of our business and the redesign of our company website. This was a big deal for us. The site was an essential part of our growth plan and would not only be the center of our e-commerce but also connect our social media, online media, and offline sales and marketing.

Before the unveiling of the redesign, the dot-com rep presented a chart plotting the progress of the dot-com side: a nice long arrow that ran from the lower left corner to the upper right. Growth! However, at one very recent point on the graph that had been artfully made as small as possible, it plunged to zero and then continued back up. Not low—*zero*.

Normally, I like to drive an agenda in my meetings to keep them focused and on schedule, but this was not my meeting. So I just listened. Now, I believe listening is an essential skill for a leader and change agent. But I also understood the agenda for this meeting was about the past and future growth of our dot-com. A drop in revenue to zero seemed too important to ignore. We all saw it, and no one was saying anything. It annoyed me. It looked to me like a big, smelly elephant in the room.

So I stopped listening, and when they said goodbye to that slide, I spoke up just like the guy in the cartoon.

"Hold on. Go back. I want to talk about that slide some more."

"We're done with that slide, and we need to move on. We don't want to talk about that."

What? Change agent vs. obstructionist Thunderdome. Two will enter. Only one can win.

"What?" I said. "You asked for my input, and I want to talk about that."

I showed no sign of wavering. The presenter showed the slide again.

Whether you are changing a brick-and-mortar firm or an online company (or something in between), you will need everything from simple facelifts to wholesale redesign. Your goal during those changes is to keep things going as much as possible. Even if you need to scale back, the business must not stop unless that business or part of it is being killed for good. This is especially true on the Web. Choosing to reinvent the wheel and build a site from scratch is hard enough (and usually unnecessary—a facelift and a few added features are usually enough to keep it breathing). But the *worst* decision is to take a site offline while those changes are implemented.

And that was clearly what had happened there. I hoped it wasn't. But it was. Oh. My. Lord. I had the elephant in my crosshairs. I kept going.

"Why did we do that? Why did we shut it down, and who made that decision?"

I didn't know that the person was in the room and was senior to me. It did not matter. This was something that needed to be said to a team that had made a boneheaded decision that had cost us money and must not happen again. I could not worry about how I was saying it or that it might get me into bigger trouble than I usually get into from running my mouth. That's the risk you take when you deal with elephants. Thus, I continued.

"I think this was a really stupid move and decision, and I hope we don't do that again. What idiot made that decision?"

Yeah, I could have said that last part better, but it was much better to have this conversation now rather than later, when more zeros appeared. It's a better way even if you're not the smartest in the room or the most tactful at conveying what needs to be said.

So talk about those elephants, people. They're there. I don't care if it is one ugly elephant sitting right there on your desk or a herd of them stampeding through your office (at bad companies, the herd finishes stampeding and then grazes happily on the bottom line). What's happening right in front of you, looming in the room so everyone sees it, but no one says anything? Cash flow? Availability of capital? Ability of the team to deliver? Revenue forecasts? I worked with a company that needed to declare Chapter 11 bankruptcy in order to survive and could not acknowledge it. Talk about an elephant!

Change agents must always ask, "What am I not seeing?" Don't feel uncomfortable—it's your job to cause tension and to ask and answer the hardest questions to solve the problems now and prevent them in the future. (*The Mirror Test* has a list of my top 20 questions to ask about your business.) Find the biggest sticking points, and lay bare the biggest holes and important topics so nothing is missed or left unsaid and unaddressed. Don't cover up! Tell your team to raise their hands and say something. Tell them to be forceful and direct. Be honest. Tell them it is a risk and they might get trampled initially, but they are not trying to win popularity contests. In the end they will come out unscathed. It's better than an "I told you so" and a bunch of finger-pointing and blame down the road.

Chapter 14

Process makes perfect! Corporate cultures are hard to change. Change processes first. Speed is good, but FAST is better.

"It's not that Jeff doesn't care about ideas; it's just that he knows those are by-products of performing the CMO job as a true leader." That's what FastCompany.com's Drew Neisser wrote about me, and what that means is, it all comes down to process. Some people get caught up in the idea rather than the process, but I think the process leads to the idea.

Change agents know what most business leaders often find out the hard way: when companies are growing rapidly and changing dramatically, things can easily go awry. That's why change agents, *before* they shake things up, like to get things under control. I may be Mr. Contrarian, the guy who challenges the accepted wisdom, strives to change everything, and likes to talk about the elephants in the room. But I am completely committed to putting systematic processes in place as part of driving change. Why? *Because I don't want to think about operations all the time. I don't want to keep thinking about process. I want to put it in place and move on.*

For a variety of reasons, my idea of process is often not an easy sell. Some companies think their current processes work just fine—even if they can't articulate clearly just what those processes might be. Sometimes my processes are viewed as old-fashioned—but some of the best things in life, like ice cream or a good steak, usually are. Some tell me they don't want to be "limited" by process, but I've seen chickens running with their heads cut off. Is that what you want for your company?

It is vitally important that you get your team aligned and in agreement regarding your goals, methods, and metrics in a way that works for you, your company, and what you stand for. Whether you are innovating with new products and services, tapping new technologies, or shifting a brand and its image, corporate change and a transformation of your business model are hard enough to manage without having a model for managing the operations that support those innovations. No identifiable call to action to rally your people. No way for them to remember what you stand for.

Business leaders must look inside their companies and give everyone a common rallying point. The foundation for this is not found in data analysis or the deployment of new technologies. And you can't just "create" a culture by saying, "This is what it is." Corporate culture is made up of too many different parts and is created over time. But operations are different. That's what you can change first and then say, "This is how we respond together" to drive the change.

Whether I'm building a team of motivated marketers, smooth salespeople, or anything else, my first job is not getting them to sell the product; it's developing the process so they can work together. I don't care if your team consists of two or two thousand, if they're not working together, the game is over. It doesn't matter what your product is. It doesn't matter how many fancy charts and reports you have. It doesn't matter if you have slick brochures and a colorful website and a million social media connections.

If you don't have an enthusiastic, dedicated team, all of whose members are working from the same playbook—if your processes suck—you've already lost. With good processes, everyone will always know if the team is in alignment with your goals and how far it's come or fallen. People become more responsible and accountable for the promises the company makes.

Processes provide a framework for change. They are about getting the work done efficiently and smartly so everyone can take responsibility for thinking big and then growing bigger. They allow you to innovate and adapt without destroying who you are. Companies that have processes in place can focus on the present *and* the future, even as they enter into the unknown. They will always succeed in the long run over companies with a bunch of headless chickens.

But remember: when establishing a process, apply the principle of Occam's razor—one simple solution is often the best and right solution. If you have too many procedures that don't empower employees or if the process is too complex, you inhibit speed.

Whether I owned a small business or led a team of thousands, I have put a process in place, usually creating an acronym to help my people and me remember the parts of the process. In *The Mirror Test*, I talked about my process for understanding value and asking questions: RACE (Research, Action, Communicate, Evaluate). When I worked at Cenveo, we created a process called SOAR (Superior operations, One company, Align resources, Replicate success). SOAR focused on our values, challenges, mission, and objectives and specifically improved key measurements for safety and customer service; meeting financial commitments; having satisfied, productive, and mobilized employees; creating total customer solutions; matching resources with customer needs; standardizing key processes; sharing best practices; and continuously looking for cost improvements.

My favorite organizing principle is a modified version of my friend Tom White's Profoundly Simple (http://profoundly simple.com) FAST system: Focus, Accountability, Speed, Trust. Tom is the steward of FAST, and he worked with me to adapt it for and integrate it into several companies, including Kodak.

- *Focus.* Clear vision, values, and principles and priorities consistent with our goals: What do we have to accomplish? What promises are we delivering on?

- *Accountability.* What is *my* promise to the company, customers, and community? Shared ownership of results, actions linked to goals, and recognizing and rewarding success.

- *Simplicity.* How do you make what you do as simple as possible so you can move quickly? Timely response, innovative solutions, and removal of obstacles.

- *Trust.* How do you engender trust among a group of diverse people who must move quickly *together*? Exceed expectations, communicate clearly, and genuinely encourage healthy debate.

To me, FAST is more than an operations process; it is a mindset. It is about keeping promises. It is about treating everyone as a customer—employees, vendors, customers, and partners—and focusing on understanding their needs, delivering on promises without excuses, embracing innovation, and continuously exceeding expectations. A process like FAST is a clear road map for operational success. It focuses on the company's goals and holds the team accountable for and cheerleads for the achievement of those goals.

For example, at Kodak, we strove for an exceptional customer experience, excellence in execution, elimination of waste and redundancy, exceeding revenue growth and profitability expectations, and engendering employee pride and passion. Employees had to understand those goals, do all they could to meet or exceed them, and communicate ideas for improvement without hesitation. FAST showed them the way. Those who followed became ambassadors for change. Those who did not: we love you, we'll miss you, goodbye.

FAST allowed my businesses to dump outdated operating procedures and marketing models and adopt new ones that fit the current business. Over time, it helped reshape our company cultures for the better. Even when we screwed up, we said let's do it FAST-er!

That's why I like to say, speed is good, but FAST is better.

Still, it took me more than a year to sell FAST at Kodak. Heck, even at my own companies, a "simple" solution like FAST was easier said than done. Just remember what my friend told me about his mother's pasta sauce: she used only five ingredients, but it took all day to prep and simmer before it was ready. It is the same story in business operations. People are often set in their ways; you can make a simple change, but it needs time to work.

Then again, change agents must also be willing to listen and adapt, and not be so set in *their* ways in the face of reasonable resistance. If you look carefully, I *adapted* Tom White's FAST. His S is for "Speed," but at Kodak we changed it to "Simplicity" because my CFO said he liked the concept, but "don't we need to make things simpler around this place?" I agreed, and we changed it in midstream—for the better. Now that is FAST!

Change means fundamental transformation. When everything from business models to products, services, and technologies to the culture and brand image is changing, a process allows leaders to focus and free their minds. Yes, processes sometimes sound corny, but there is a reason they have been around forever: they are serious business—they work. Find one that works for you!

Chapter 15

Change your tune and be pitch perfect: hook me in 8 seconds (the lean-in factor); sell me in 110 seconds (close the deal). What's your 118?

One of the signature features of *The Mirror Test* was the creation of the 118—my modern version of the elevator pitch. I have always liked the idea of the elevator pitch (i.e., being able to pitch yourself and what your company offers in the span of an elevator ride). But like so many old-but-worthy ideas, the elevator pitch has become too slow for our times. It even *sounds* slow for an age in which speed and immediate relevance are essential in pitching. Technology has made everything (including elevators!) move faster: no more than 2 minutes and sometimes as little as 30 seconds for an average ride these days.

That's why I created the 118. That's the number of seconds you actually have to pitch to me: 8 seconds to hook me and up to 110 seconds to reel me in. Those first 8 seconds are the key, though. In researching the idea, my writer Jim and I discovered that the length of time the average human can concentrate on something and not lose some focus is as little as 8 seconds. Eight! (It's true—we found it on the Internet!) Thirty seconds, then, was way too long for getting that lean-in factor for your pitch. You know how you hear something in a conversation and you lean in because you want to hear the rest of it? That's what you want from your prospect in those first 8 seconds of the 118.

Eight seconds is also the length of time for a qualified ride in professional bull riding. You must hold on as one of the world's meanest, toughest animals tries to throw you off—just as any business prospect will. Thus, in the first 8 seconds of the 118, you must be strong and focused as well as compelling in order to succeed. Hold on tight! You must get prospects to lean in *and* hold their attention. Make it in those 8 seconds, and they'll give you 110 more to drive your message home with no bull. But if you have not sold them at the end of the 110 seconds, they will start to tune out. At that point, you are either moving forward or not.

The response to my idea of and the need for a 118 was tremendous. From the stage, inside companies, on blogs, even on my own website and social media pages where we ran contests for the best 118s, people acknowledged its power and possibility. *That's why I am so surprised at how bad so many of them still are.* That's if a business even has one!

Honestly, I expected more of them to be good. I expected more leaders to be able to pull them off. This is the one thing that encapsulates everything about your business and you. Grab my attention and close me! Why wouldn't I expect this to be the best thing you do? Yet even by old-fashioned elevator pitch standards, they were bad.

The worst is the name-dropping. Getting me to lean in and then selling me on the value you provide requires more than rattling off that you worked with Pepsi or Coke, Dell or Apple,

Kodak or Canon. Those are just names. They mean nothing to my business and me; I could give a rat's behind. Besides, do you really think there's anyone out there who hasn't worked with some Big Important Company? In my experience, everyone can name-drop—what's in it for me?

Instead, during your 118, deliver one compelling story about you or your business that is relevant to me, conveys your value, and convinces me with specifics why I should do business with you. Most of the time, you get one shot. Why blow it with a bad one? Businesses that have this down are hugely successful every time they change and grow. They have brand champions who trust and believe in who they are, both within their companies and at their customers and vendors, too.

Simply put, most leaders haven't sat down and fundamentally focused on the DNA—the very core—of their business. What makes you special? What is it that makes you *you*? What connects you with your customers? Part of my positioning is to say to potential customers, "Are you interested in being a high-growth company? I only work with high-growth companies." Right away that makes them think about who they are. Usually, they tell me they are high growth, so I say, "Maybe I can work with you. Show me you how you're growing." We're already moving toward a sale together.

Your 118 should also describe the thing that separates you from everyone else that sells the same thing. I don't care what businesses you are in or what other services you offer—how are you different, and how do you convey it? What's your story, and how does that story connect to your prospects? Sadly, even companies that can tell their stories do so only from their own perspective—the way they're used to telling them or have always told them. In working with people and companies that needed to change, I saw them constantly slip back into "old speak" and old habits about what they do and how they do it, with static, canned, self-centered PowerPoint presentations that told no story and had zero sense of what to do in those 118 seconds.

Leaders need to get away from bland pronouncements that say "we do this" and focus on "what we do for you." You're supposed to understand not just what you're selling, but what it offers to your prospect. For example, I worked with a mobile company on its 118, and we decided the whole mobile experience reminded us of one of the greatest opportunities of all time: the Oklahoma Land Rush. So, why not describe it like that? Mobile is like the Oklahoma Land Rush. Describe the scene: tens of thousands of hopeful settlers, all looking to lay their hands on a piece of land and strike it rich; some have horses, some have wagons, and some are on foot. Those who choose the right opportunities will win the rush. Now connect this to your prospect: we partner with you to navigate these opportunities and stake your claim. List the benefits. Show you know the way to go, how to pick the right platforms, and how to make the right decisions.

Did the company ending up using this analogy? Actually, no. It found another story that worked even better. But it had gone beyond starting with a bland, empty pronouncement like that last sentence in the previous paragraph: "We know the way to go, how to pick the right platforms, and how to make the right decisions." Start there and your prospects will say, "Yeah, who doesn't?" Paint them that picture of what they are facing first, and that same line will demonstrate a deep understanding of the landscape and what they need.

So, kill the slides and the long presentations and create your 118. *Now*. And once you have that 118, make sure everyone in your company, from top to bottom, knows it and says proudly, "This is what we are today." Get alignment around what it is you deliver, because business can happen anywhere with anyone these days, and if you're bad at it, chances are your people are clueless. Too often, I'll talk to the employees of the companies I work with and for, and I can't find a common thread when I ask, "What do you do?" I feel like I'm on an endless version of *The Newlywed Game*, where couples seem to know nothing about each other, but at least those people were sleeping together!

At Kodak, I would ask people, "What are we as a company? What is it we do?" Many (oh, so many) would respond, "We're a film company." "Well, if we're a film company," I replied, "we're dead. That's not because Kodak doesn't do billions of dollars in film anymore. That's still not what we *do*. That's what we *make*."

Think about this way: does McDonald's sell the Happy or the Meal? Kodak wasn't about its cameras or its film or its printers. That's not what made us dominant in any market, past or present. Kodak was about how those products made you feel about what it did. Our products made things that people would run into a burning building to save. That was the core of Kodak: emotional technology, or what I called M^3I^2: we help people to make, manage, and move images and information in their homes and businesses. "That's what we do," I told people. That's what Kodak was passionate about: the emotional technology that goes into every product and everything we do and make. That's the value we offered. That's what everyone in the company needed to feel so that we all could sell it every day.

It may sound contradictory to say that companies are successful at changing when they get back to their core, but it is not. Getting back to your core principles makes it possible to embrace change! You have to know who you are so you can change in the right direction. It doesn't matter what business you are in. You use the same principles to sell a box of soap, a political candidate, a university, software technology, biotech equipment . . . any house, no matter how big, needs a strong foundation.

Chapter 16

Mastering your 118 (a.k.a. elevator pitch 2.0): a step-by-step primer

WHAT IS A 118?

A 118 is my twenty-first-century version of what some people used to call the elevator pitch, an out-of-date name for a worthy idea that you must sell what your company offers (and yourself) in the span of an elevator ride. The name comes from the 118 seconds you actually have to pitch a prospect: 8 seconds to hook 'em and up to 110 seconds to reel 'em in.

What You Must Do in That 118 Seconds

- Grab the attention of your prospect, be it a client, investor, or potential employee.

- Convey who you are.

- Describe what your business offers.

- Explain the promises you will deliver on.

Why You Need a 118

You need speed and immediate relevance. A compelling, attention-grabbing 118 presents who you are and the value of what you do and sells that to anyone, internally and externally. Used correctly, it can only help your business grow bigger.

Got It—What's Next?

Follow the four steps given here to create a 118 that works for your business.

Step 1: Create the First 8 and Grab Your Prospect's Attention

The first 8 seconds are the most important part of your entire pitch. That's when you grab the attention of your prospect. If you do not connect in the first 8 seconds, then you probably will not have her attention for the remaining 110. This is a great time to compliment something the prospect has done recently and show how you complement her business or at least know what it is that she does.

- *The Good:* Mentions your product or service and tells how it will help your prospect. "In less than two minutes, I will tell you how the use of [me, my company, my service] will grow your development department 115 percent."

- *The Bad:* Mentions what you're offering, but lacks any reference to what it offers your prospect. "My name is Sam Maybe-Somebody, and my company The Hopeful-WhoKnows wants to work with your company using our WeThinkSuperService."

- *The Ugly:* Makes no mention of your company or service and how the prospect will benefit. "My name is Sam Nobody, and my company wants to work with your company because we think we can help you."

Step 2: Convey Who You Are—the *Real* You

Let your prospects know who you are. They want you to tell them what it is you do most passionately. Do not waste time telling them whom you work with or for—they need to know who you are. This is not the time to drop the names of people and companies you've worked for in the past, and it is definitely not the time to mention any negative moments in your career. Talk about your passion and excellence.

- *The Good:* Mentions your experience without name-dropping and shares your passion for work that connects to what your prospect needs. "For 15 years, I have lived my passion for designing the most cost-efficient communication systems in the business."

- *The Bad:* Briefly mentions your experience and previous responsibilities, but focuses on the previous organization. "For 15 years, I developed communications systems for Zapidio Communications, which focuses on university communication systems."

- *The Ugly:* Mentions your previous company and a negative outcome. Does not mention your specific area of expertise. "I used to work for Zapidio Communications and then I was downsized, and I'm looking for freelance work in the communications field."

Step 3: Describe What Your Business Offers

Let your prospects know who or what your business is. Your prospects want you to tell them what you do better than anyone else. What is your bottom line? Why do they need this information? Provide specifics of what your company does and why you're the best in the business for the specific needs of your prospects. If you're pitching marketing expertise, pitch marketing expertise and table discussing your other strengths until later.

- *The Good:* Has specific details about why your company is effective and the best at what it does. "My company increases the customer satisfaction ratings of struggling companies by using the power of technology to communicate effectively and efficiently through e-mail, social media, and Twitter."

- *The Bad:* Briefly mentions what your company does, but not specifically enough to address what the prospect needs. "My company works with other companies to help them communicate better with their customers using technology like social media and e-mail."

- *The Ugly:* Vaguely refers to what your company does, but with no mention of how it will benefit your prospect. "My company works with other companies to help them communicate better with the people they work with."

Step 4: Explain the Promises on Which You Will Deliver

Your prospects want more specifics on what your brand offers. Remember: a brand is nothing more than a promise delivered. So what promise are you offering to deliver on for them? Know your audience and its bottom line. Steer clear of saying that you will create buzz for your prospects, because if the bottom line is not measurable (sales is *not* buzz) or directly beneficial to the prospects, then they will have no interest in anything you're proposing.

- *The Good:* Has specific details and knowledge about what your company can do for the prospect. "After reviewing the last two quarters of sales from your online Web development company, we believe the use of our social media networking program will increase your sales by 25 percent in the next quarter."

- *The Bad:* Shows limited knowledge of the prospect's needs and offers a brief idea of what area you desire to work with. "I've been watching your company on the news, and I think that the use of our new machine could increase your production rates."

- *The Ugly:* Does not know what the prospect's needs are and makes no reference to your expertise—only broad and overly general platitudes. "Our company will work hard to address any and every need that you have to grow your company."

Great! Anything Else?

Yes; get thee to a mirror and polish your 118. Look in that mirror and recite it as often as you can so that when opportunity knocks, you can open the door and sell, sell, sell. I don't mean memorize it. That just sounds rehearsed or canned. What I mean is drink your own Kool-Aid until it oozes through your body and comes out every pore as utter confidence and belief in who you are, what you are selling, and how it connects to your prospects. Let everyone see your passion. Get out there and *use* it.

Friendsourcing Controlling the Mission

As I finish the manuscript for this book, it has been a little more than a year since *The Mirror Test* came out and I officially left Kodak. I spent much of that first year setting up my New York office, speaking at meetings and conferences, consulting, and pitching and lining up new clients. Except for holidays and my son's wedding, I have not slowed down much personally and less so professionally. Changes and opportunities were happening simultaneously, quickly, and furiously. I could manage or handle some of it, but my failed efforts at cloning meant I needed my people to sell *us*, not just me. And I wanted them to. So I needed to make the time and enable them to do so.

So as my company headed into its first annual summit following the publication of this book, I decided to host a friendly competition to create the next Hayzlett 118. I challenged the team to work together in groups to create and then pitch me their versions of our corporate 118. After all, it is my business's core—its DNA—but unlike real DNA (at least so far), you can and often must reshape and redesign it. Doing so makes for great team building. Clark Kokich told me he did something similar in building and growing Razorfish: "We decreed for two years there would be no debate on the 'What?' but infinite debate on the 'How?' In other words, we agreed as a group we would stay focused 100 percent on our strategic goal, never letting anyone question the direction, but we gave everyone complete authority to debate how we should get there. This created a collaborative culture where people were working together to drive change through the organization."

In Razorfish's case, the "what" is the conditions of satisfaction for the company, but the "how" is the 118, and that how is what connects your people from top to bottom to the changes you are driving and the mission they support—especially their connection to the first 8 seconds. As Porter Gale, vice president of marketing at Virgin America, told me, "A companywide focus on the mission to create 'an airline that people love' was at the heart of our driving change during the development and operation of Virgin America."

Nothing made me smile more than seeing my team collaborate and really engage our 118. It is engaging and empowering for them, it will help me know what they don't know, and it will help me see what I might be missing in my own company and eventually weed out the people who just don't get it. I look forward to pitching you our latest 118 soon!

Chapter 17

Just because you killed a cow doesn't mean you're gonna eat steak for dinner. There's lots of messy work to do, and none of it is easy.

Shout "Change!" in a crowded movie house and people will ignore you, shush you, or flip you off. That's true in business, too. Knowing you must change, believing you can change, and screaming you will change—even starting to change— doesn't mean you'll get everything you want immediately. Change is a mentality and a process that takes work. You can ask the right questions, have the right attitude, know your conditions of satisfaction, and identify the next steps, but all this means nothing if you can't push forward through all the inevitable messiness.

Field dressing a cow is a perfect analogy for understanding what I mean. I've dressed rabbits, squirrels, pheasants (lots of pheasants), deer, and elk. Change, however, is most like dressing a cow—the biggest animal most people will ever do. (You may need to talk about elephants in the room, but it's a lot easier to field-dress a metaphor.) Killing the cow is just the beginning. Killing it only leaves it dead on the ground. To get what you want, you need to field-dress it. A lot goes into that dressing. Bleeding the cow only hints at what is to come. This might be graphic and hard to hear—sorry, vegetarians and people who think steak comes from happy cows who are grazing in pastures with their sides missing—but so is change.

You start by cutting into the cavity to clean it out and cool down the meat. You need a super-sharp knife to cut through the hide. But don't cut too deep or you will cut into the stomach cavity and the intestines and everything inside will spill out, ruining the meat it touches. After cutting, you start cleaning out the cavity, and *wow* you should see the steaming mess that comes out: intestines and stomachs (all four of them) along with all the organs. This stuff is important (and in some cases delicious)— the vital inner workings of the cow—and it must be cleaned out quickly, carefully, and respectfully. It also looks like crap because it *is literally* full of crap—God forbid you cut the intestines or nick the bladder, as feces and urine will pour out on your shoes if you do. Once you expose and start to deal with the innards, you also need to reach your arms all the way into the heat of the cavity, grab hold of the esophagus with both hands, and pull and pull and pull until it releases. Oh, and before you get started, don't forget to break the pelvic bone by hacking at it or jumping on it until it breaks. And did I mention carving out the rectum?

Congratulations, you just finished Step 1.

Step 2 starts with separating the hide from the animal. This takes time for even the most experienced dressers because—unless you want to be wasteful—you need to keep that hide looking its best so it can be turned into leather or a rug. So you must cut close enough to the hide but not through it, but also far enough away from the meat underneath so you don't lose any good meat against the hide.

Okay, well done. On to Step 3.

Time to start dividing up the cow into the cuts you want and need. But wait! No one can eat a whole cow, not even me! So before you cut, you must know what parts are what and identify them on your cow. For example, do you know where the best and most expensive strip of meat—the tenderloin—is? Don't go by look or position on the body. (The tenderloin is near the back.) You must also know the parts that you want *and* those that the people who will be sharing the cow with you want. You may want all thick-cut sirloins, but you might have more demand for whole roasts and ground beef. *Now*, you can start quartering and cutting.

You can see the finish line, but things are still not easy or neat. The blood is all over you. One mistake can destroy a cut and lower its value. If you move too slowly, your meat can start to spoil. But Step 4 is at least the last step in the field: packaging. You need to wrap it all up and get it into the freezer and ready to go. And what does that leave you? Raw meat. You still have one step left; you *still* need to decide how to cook it!

If you need a moment after reading all this, I understand. But I warn you: the process of change is every bit as messy as this sounds, and the possibilities are every bit as delightful. If you can have the change agent attitude and can commit to changing (the kill) and dealing with the process (dressing)—if you can deal with your operations and people (the guts), the mood and the way you look (the hide), and the goals, strategies, and tactics for your products and services (the meat), and then package it right, your change will lead to growth (a steak dinner).

If this does not appeal to you, don't kill the cow. Why bother? To get what you want, you will need to do this, and changing a business, like killing a cow, is never easy. Walk away and do something else. If it were easy, everybody would have done it.

When I'm standing in front of a mountainous seafood buffet in Las Vegas or a bubbling lobster tank in South Dakota, I'm constantly amazed at the communication, infrastructure, logistics, and technology required to get the stuff there. Good leaders understand and can process the details of all these pieces in their businesses in a millisecond. They've been down the road before; they get it. They can think through all the steps. If you don't have this ability, read on and learn to diagram it out like the parts of the cow . . . okay, fish, chicken, cauliflower, or whatever. Learn how and why it all works, and know what needs to be done.

You killed the cow—great, you're thinking big. But growing bigger? Well, that's what's next.

Friendsourcing Cow Killing

I love the way some of my friends reacted when I told them the title of this chapter and asked what they thought it meant. Some were confused. Others preferred to think about "sacred cows" (which, like elephants in the room, are important to deal with, but are much easier to field-dress). Some couldn't even bear to answer me because they were vegetarians. My agent, Wendy Keller of Keller Media, Inc., tried to answer, but then had one word for me: "Gross!" Should I have said, "Just because you planted the carrots doesn't mean you'll get soup," or, "Just because you slay the broccoli doesn't mean you'll have quiche"?

I guess my friend Russ Mann, CEO of Covario, was right when he said, "The short answer is: if you want to enjoy your steak dinner in business, be prepared to offend the vegetarians." Actually Russ didn't know about the other responses when he said this to me. He was talking about getting so focused on parts of the how—killing the cow, preparing the steak dinner, and wondering if the people you are dealing with really want steak in the first place—that you forget about all of the process and the dinner never gets served: "There's a lot of pressure on CEOs to do things 'just so.' You can't be too aggressive and abrasive, but you can't be too soft or touchy-feely. You need to be the humble servant leader and the charismatic visionary at the same time."

What Tammy McCrary, an entertainment executive, said resonated with me in the same way when she talked about killing as the first step: "It's the idea. And there have been many great ones. However, to get your business's product (the steak dinner), there are specific steps (how it is prepared and served) that have to be carried out to arrive at that product. Unfortunately, more often than not, those steps are not done and you miss out on achieving the product goal." Or as Clark Kokich, chairman of Razorfish, mused as he connected my line to his customers: "We tend to overcelebrate the 'hunters' in business and undercelebrate the 'farmers.' Winning customers is a small part of the job. Nurturing, caring for, and growing customers are what get the steak dinner."

When we were shooting the pilot for a TV show, I consulted with a gym that was in horrible shape. We spent an exhausting couple of days evaluating what sucked, fixing the place up, firing people to improve the mood, talking about elephants in the room (which for this gym included bankruptcy), and getting people's heads in the right place about change. We killed the cow! But as my friend Joe Pulizzi, content marketing evangelist, said about cow killing, "You can't half-ass your business. You go all in or you go home."

Sure you can "dress" your change differently, but you can never stop at the kill, leave out steps, or just take what you want and ignore the mess on the ground. Those kinds of shortcuts are shameful, disrespectful, reckless, thoughtless, superficial, and inefficient. Plus, the process will *still* be messy and you *still* won't get to do everything the way you want.

Many of my friends have different ways of saying this. Ronn Torossian, CEO of 5W Public Relations, says about killing cows, "One plus one doesn't necessarily equal two in business. Many things can get in the way, and having a business plan or some kind of abstract business valuation doesn't mean anything in the real business world. Perseverance and sheer determina-tion matter tremendously." Miles Young, chief executive officer at Ogilvy & Mather Worldwide, prefers to look at it this way: "If you kill a cow, you deserve to eat it at dinnertime. But so often, execution gets in the way."

So do surprises. Eric Mower, chairman and chief execu-tive officer of Eric Mower and Associates, noted, "So much is out of our control. Things change. Surprises happen. Disap-pointments abound. The best-laid plans in business—just as in war—go awry. That's life." Keith Larson, president of structurIT WorldWide, felt the same way: "There are always surprises in business. One time, at my previous company, I was given new sales targets to help the company be successful. I accepted the challenge and, like a good corporate soldier, got the new sales from present customers. I was not successful, though, because I was then told that the company wanted new sales from *new* cus-tomers. I assumed that my approach would be successful, but assuming in business is bad business."

Just remember: there's no way you're going to get it all right the first time. Probably not the second or third time either, and that's okay. Like I said, nothing is easy, and no one's going to die (except the cow). But I promise you'll get more organized and efficient every time you try. After all, one properly field-dressed cow is enough to get many delicious dinners on the table. But eventually you will run out of food and have to start the process all over again. As Kent Huffman, chief marketing of-ficer at BearCom Wireless Worldwide, said, "Steak for dinner in the business world is all about focus, discipline, and results. You have to be able to pinpoint the right strategy, develop the most appropriate tactics and processes, and then stick with it until you can deliver measurable, repeatable results." Mike Steinberg, president and CEO of Relyco: Printing & Payment Solutions, concurs: "One big deal does not necessarily equal success. It may feel great for a time, but you must find a way to continually win. By staying current and looking to the future, we are striving to be consistent in our growth and success. We don't look at success one cow at time. Success to us is continually growing our business every day, week, month, quarter, year . . ."

They're right—everyone I quoted here is. Because killing the cow and getting steak on the table for dinner is about the *whole* process—it's about the space in driving change between thinking big and growing bigger.

Part Two

Grow Bigger

Starting and Sustaining Momentum

Chapter 18

Never approach a bull from the front, a horse from the back, or a fool from any direction. And don't squat with your spurs on!

Now that we have talked about killing a cow, let's start the second part of our change process by my telling you a little something about cow tipping: it doesn't exist. Cow tipping? It's never been done. First of all, cows don't sleep standing up. Second of all, even if they did, what makes you think you could tip them? They're huge. I can't even move one when it's *dead*, let alone when it can resist. And finally, even if you had people with the strength to tip a cow, what makes you think it wouldn't walk away before you could tip it?

Simply put, anyone who tells you he tipped a cow is lying, and anyone who believes in cow tipping is a fool. And all this foolish talk reminds me of the time I was on a panel with some chief marketing officers talking about creating your 118 when one of the panelists turned to me and said, "Why do you even need to pitch at all?"

Huh? I turned to him and answered, without hesitating, "What are you smokin'? Nothing sells itself forever."

Okay, maybe I could have said that in a nicer way. No, wait; I couldn't. The fact is, he was serious, and so was I. No one wakes up and says, "I can't wait to be stupid," but that's what this sounded like to me: stupid. What makes people think that they can stop pitching? It sounded like something said by people who don't sell stuff! It sounded like it came from someone who believes in cow tipping.

It's true, you should not lead with your product when you're pitching it. (That's part of the point of the 118.) And yes, maybe for iPhone-like products, there comes a point where businesses *seemingly* don't need to pitch those products. Some of the best pitches for the most trusted brands can sell their products through desire or emotional connections without ever mentioning the product. (They just show how that product fits perfectly into our lifestyle—they reach out and touch someone!) But this is still pitching.

Whether the pitch is in-your-face or subtle, targeted to thousands or to millions, business-to-business or consumer-targeted, off- or online, a business must make the effort to market and sell itself, or it will die. That's the only way to grow bigger. What's the point of making all those big thinking changes to your attitude and your internal systems if you can't get out there and sell yourself every day and through everything you do? Selling is not a negative term, just as change is not a goal in itself, but rather a chance to build on success to create a bigger future for a business. Be smart but relentless in leading the change you want by creating great pitches and plans, and then beat the competition with awesome service and responsiveness. Change offers a chance for businesses to see their markets and their customers in new ways—a chance to consider new strategies, investigate and invest in new technologies, invent new ways of doing business, test things, and more. It's about opportunity; that's what's most appealing about it.

But to capitalize on these opportunities and grow, businesses *always* need to be selling themselves and the changes they are making through everything they do. It's just common sense, and not doing it is like squatting with spurs on. You *can* do it, but it's gonna leave a mark. In other words, be smart or get stuck. Nothing sells itself forever. Don't squat with your spurs on: never stop selling your company . . . and *yourself!* Which reminds me of another of my favorite cowboy expressions that's perfect for this point as well: never approach a bull from the front, a horse from the back, or a fool from any direction. In business, the bull is your competition, the horse is your team, and the fools are the people who stand in your way—and you if you let them!

Let's consider your competition, the mighty bull. Bulls are awesome, powerful, well-bred, huge, and nasty. Bulls will always try to oppose you. Think you can come at a bull head-on? That's crazy stupid and dangerous—and potentially *really costly*. First of all, *they can see you*. Most of them are already planning what they will do when you come at them head-on. If you do that, all it does is give them time to get ready to knock you down. To hit you. To drain you of your resources. To gore you. Do what a bullfighter does instead: distract them with a red cape and then approach them from the side and put the sword in them. But remember: even the best bullfighters never engage a bull that is fully charged and ready to fight; they have clowns and other helpers who distract the bulls and wear them down before the battle. If you don't have that option, at the very least, sneak up on them. Stay downwind of them, stalk them, and come at them from a direction they don't expect, then attack them before they know what hit them.

And then have your team of "horses" ready to respond. Approach your horses from the front and tell them everything they need to know to be prepared for what is to come. That's what you must do. Why would you want to tell your team where you're going in hindsight? I want my people to know right from the beginning where we are going. Sneak up on horses or people from behind, and they are going to kick you. They are going to flee. Their natural tendency is to run when they are surprised. So tell 'em right up front and look them in the eye—it may result in resistance, but not fear.

And fools? Let 'em go or let 'em drive themselves off a cliff. Don't "suffer fools gladly, seeing ye yourselves are wise"—some people and situations just can't be fixed. If you lead a horse (an idea, an employee, a perennially unhappy customer) to water and it won't drink, don't hit it. Get rid of it!

Try to keep this cowboy business wisdom in mind as you change and grow bigger. It will surely be useful on this next part of the trail because growing bigger is a lot like a gold rush; only those in the first wave ever strike gold. Those that don't can make money selling maps and tools, girls and grub to the second wave. So, can your business find new gold, or are you digging where too many others have already staked their claim? Can you make money selling "maps and tools" to the late arrivals or specific customers? Should you explore new frontiers to grow your brand, and can you do so without breaking the promises of that brand? And when the rush is over, how do you know whether to move on or get out completely?

As you grow bigger, those are just some of the questions you need to answer. And the best way for me to help you start answering those questions is through the lens of a product that's worth *more* than gold: printer ink.

Friendsourcing Getting Thrown from the Saddle

"Go to the tool shed and get me my quarter-inch socket wrench with a ⅞-inch blah blah blah." I was 10 years old, and my dad had just told me to do something. That meant: don't ask questions; do it now! The only problem was that "blah blah blah" part. What had he said? I remember going back to the shed, looking at all those tools, and not knowing what I was supposed to bring. So I folded up the entire gray metal toolbox, which easily weighed more than I did, and lugged it between my legs as I shuffled back to the house. At least I knew I'd have the right tool that day. But in business as in life, you can't always lug your toolbox with you, and even if you could, you will still make mistakes in trying to grow bigger.

Like every cowboy, every change agent will get thrown from the saddle at least once. How do I know? *Every* change agent I talked to for this book told me so. Maybe the saddle was somehow loose (the implementation was shaky), the horse tripped (the team fell down or fell apart), or something hit them hard (the competition proved more resilient or aggressive than they expected). But in business, whether you fall forward, backward, or straight off the side of the saddle, it's *still* not likely you'll get really badly hurt. Because what have we learned about mistakes like these? No one is going to die.

Kevin M. Joyce, chief sales and marketing officer at Miranda Technologies, didn't die when he found himself "excluded from the inside circle and nearly eliminated from the executive team and stepped back to understand why it had happened." He said, "I tried to objectively evaluate what I was or was not doing correctly, decide if I was willing to work with those who had lost faith in me and address the concerns they had, or if I should say, 'Bug off,' lick my wounds, and go elsewhere." He stayed and made change happen.

Clark Kokich, chairman of Razorfish, didn't die in 1996 when he left AT&T Wireless to start his own business: "Two years later I had lost $5 million of other people's money and all of my own. I was 47 years old, dead broke, and a proven loser." In fact, one of his investors asked him to join them. "I had other, less risky opportunities, but despite my recent failure, I decided to dive once more into the insanity of high-risk start-ups. It worked out pretty well."

Miles S. Nadal, chairman, founder, and CEO of MDC Partners, Inc., didn't die, even if he felt like dying, when he convinced an extraordinarily prominent investor to invest in his company and then watched his stock go down as they tried to figure out their strategy, achieve scale, and generate stable, predictable, profitable growth. "It certainly was not intentional on my part or on the part of anyone within MDC," he said. "And it wasn't just our stock that fell; it was our reputation within the investment community." He spent the next 10 years getting back on his horse, so to speak, and his company has achieved measurable success. And while he has never won that investor back, he is still trying!

Andy and Julie Plata, co-CEOs of Computer Output Print & Internet (COPI), didn't die, even though their business almost did, when new sales stopped coming into their 35-year-old software and services company: "We were staring at a potential business failure until we decided to replace 'past-thinking' employees with 'future-thinking' business builders. We also changed to a law firm–style business model, with 'partners' who are essentially independent businesses operating through our company. In hindsight, we should have more quickly identified employees who no longer fit and used our contacts and resources to locate other positions for them. This would have allowed us to stop the bleeding and get back to profitability sooner."

Slava Apel, CEO of Amazing Print Corp., didn't die when, after numerous pitches, he was about to land the biggest deal for his company and then didn't: "The contracts were drawn; investments on our part were made to make sure we could handle the business. At the eleventh hour, another 'runner-up' company ended up getting the business. It took time to get back on a horse, both emotionally and financially." The best result of his fall? "We started to appreciate the clients we had even more."

One time I wound up saddling a bloated horse. As we rode off, he exhaled, and my saddle started to roll over—with me in it! Next thing you know, I was riding upside down on my horse. That's what it must have felt like for Tammy McCrary, an entertainment executive, when she told me, "I chose the wrong partner in business. We were not aligned in vision or purpose." Tammy made the decision to get right back on her change horse: "It may take a minute to get your stride back, but I remind myself when discouragement sets in that I am a spiritual being controlling this physical universe; therefore, circumstances do not control me."

That's true even if people literally have their horses taken out from under them:

- A hostile takeover left Keith Larson, now president of structurIT Worldwide, out on the street and unable to compete in his industry for two years as part of the terms of his severance. After two years, he jumped back in, bent on revenge. But his cooler head soon prevailed: "During the two plus years of being out of the industry, many things had changed in the industry. If I had been in the industry during that time, I would have lost perspective. Sitting on the sidelines gave me a fresh look at the industry and what changes needed to take place now to be competitive in the industry."

- My agent, Wendy Keller of Keller Media, Inc., was doing great in 2007 when her house and office building both burned down in a Malibu wildfire. What did Wendy do? She "walked through bookstores and saw all the authors I'd helped and thought about all the tens of thousands of readers whose lives had been changed because of my contribution" and eventually rose from the ashes.

- Porter Gale, VP of marketing at Virgin America, was at an advertising agency that closed the office she was in and could not move her elsewhere. She decided, "Rather than sit around depressed, I consulted—shot videos, ran new business pitches, and interviewed for a client-side job when I had no client-side experience" and did not let her "fears hold [her] back from what's possible."

Enduring any of these inevitable mishaps teaches business leaders that chances are they aren't going to die from a fall or a foray into pheasant farming (just to name one of the times I was thrown from the saddle—see *The Mirror Test*). Yes, it's scary, and yes, there are consequences, but get over it and get used to it—that's the risk we take when we take the ride.

Chapter 19

Battle is the most magnificent competition in which a human being can indulge. It brings out all that is best; it removes all that is base.

The following statement will not be surprising to anyone who has met me: at Kodak, I had a team of attorneys following me around—not to close any big deals I might make, but to protect the company from the things I might say or do. I was their job security. And at no time in my tenure at Kodak did I have more attorneys following me around than when we started a battle with "Big Ink."

I'm still not allowed to name our main target. (Let's just say its initials are HP.) This company alone was making $9 billion a year in *profit* off its ink. *$9 billion!* Not the printers, the *ink*. It probably lost money on the hardware, but ink was the profit center—that was the meat you didn't give away. After all, you never see a deal for free ink, but printers are practically—and often completely— free. Heck, I could probably grab a printer and walk out of a store with it strapped to my head and no one would care. But the ink? That's locked up behind the counter or trapped in bombproof plastic cases with 10 security strips that set off alarms at corporate headquarters.

Why? Because ink by weight is more expensive than the most expensive Russian caviar. And by volume? Consider this: bottled water is more expensive than oil. Vodka, scotch, and other premium liquors top bottled water, and the best champagne tops liquor. Further up the price scale is penicillin, and that saves lives. More expensive than all of them is the ink in your inkjet printer.

Put simply, Big Ink had created a version of the classic (and effective if you can execute and sustain it) razor blade business model that Kodak knew so well. After all, for decades, Kodak had the very definition of this business model: selling customers the "razors" (cameras) they loved, but, more important, keeping them coming back to buy the "razor blades" (film). This model works in service businesses, too, where an installation or initial visit might be cheap or free, but maintenance contracts are necessary or required, and that costs money.

Big Ink had that kind of scale, where the printer was the razor, but you needed insanely expensive ink razor blades, and Kodak wanted in. In the case of film, Kodak's razor blade model collapsed when the world changed and the competition went digital. But we were not going to be able to compete with Big Ink through any technological innovation. We were going to have to compete on value—not just price, but value. We were going to market change by changing the total cost of the business. We would have to educate people about Big Ink's free printer and expensive ink model. We would need to show how Big Ink made its profits on the backs of the people.

And to do this, we were going to have to go "to war."

I always say that if you don't have an enemy, get one. Get to know that enemy, and race as fast as possible to get ahead of it. In this case, we had one, and even if you are not the son of a military man and someone who loves military history like me, you have got to see the similarities between a war and what we were about to do in business.

Let's start with the fact that to launch an attack and compete in a business like this, you need the support of your "nation." Of course, no decree in business (or politics) ever gets everyone aligned with it. There will always be people who think your way or your idea is the wrong one, even if they don't have an alternative way or idea. As we discussed, you can get input from some of those people some of the time. But in the end, someone has to make a decision, and that decision—especially in times of great change—had best be supported at and well funded from the top.

In the case of our Big Ink war, it was: the CEO had given the chief operating officer and me as chief marketing officer the task of making this a major effort. He made it clear that our jobs were riding on it. We were tied to each other. Our jobs were on the line, and we would need to work together every moment. The conditions of satisfaction were clear. We knew both the objective and how to measure our success: by the net realized rate, or NRR.

NRR is a tough, tough way to measure results for even the best change agents. Marketers like me are great at raising revenue. We know we can be successful in getting impressions and stories and write-ups. We pretty much know that about any campaign at launch. But getting down to an emphasis on margins? Oh, man, that's different. It requires a different approach from just plain marketing. To start with, it requires winning over your vendors, your salespeople, and your internal team. After all, winning is the overall goal in any battle: "No bastard ever won a war by dying for his country. He won it by making the other poor dumb bastard die for his country."

That superb last line is not mine but one that is often mistakenly attributed to General George S. Patton. Actually, George C. Scott, *playing* Patton in the movie *Patton*, said it. It's still a great line, despite that, as you now know, although the battles in business may be fierce, no one is going to die. In fact, that line is almost as good as the real Patton quote that is the title of this chapter. And I could not agree more with its description of battle, whether in war or in business: "Battle is the most magnificent competition in which a human being can indulge. It brings out all that is best; it removes all that is base."

To have my team ready for this particular battle, I decided to teach my elite team literally how to go to war. I called it "Project Patton," and it has become my field map for change agents who are heading into their own battles, showing them how to

- Prepare and anticipate needs.

- Deploy the right tactics.

- Be responsible and accountable at every turn.

- Decide how to respond and what to respond to when heading into "battle."

- Constantly report back on progress.

But the key to getting your "Project Patton" right is that first step: preparation. You cannot hope to succeed if your team is not with you and ready. Remember: approach your horses from the *front*. Educate them and lead them. Show them your conditions of satisfaction. Remember: you have spent time assembling a team that is willing, wants to, and needs to fight along with you; battle will bring out their best.

Friendsourcing Top-to-Bottom Support

I want to return to a small but important point I made earlier about Kodak's war with Big Ink: we were supported by and well funded from the top. As you will read shortly, when dealing with the reality of today's customers' needs and expectations, I always think a bottom-up approach, which empowers your customers and frontline employees, is better than the old top-down model. I want our customers and community to feel we are connecting with them and doing what we do because they said so. But of course, even a bottom-up approach needs support from the top. There has to be a mood that says we are in it together. Our battle with Big Ink took a bottom-up approach, and that meant the teams were going to make a lot of decisions on behalf of the company. They had to know that they were allowed to do so and that they had air cover from the CEO on down.

Paul Caine, executive vice president and chief revenue officer of Time Inc., knows it is important to establish this mood from the moment you set your goals: "The entire operation needs to be focused against the same goals (top to bottom). They need to be clear on the expectations, the path to get there, and the resources they need. By not being in sync, you can create a disconnect amongst the team and take everyone off strategy. Most successful teams remain aligned toward the same goal and are clear on the path."

But Keith Larson, president of structurlT Worldwide, and a friend who was with me when we created a "right-side-up organization" at Cenveo, told me another important reason change agents need that air cover. "No real long-lasting change really occurs without the buy-in and real support of the leadership. Think about it; the leaders of a company usually made it to the top of a company based on their ability to maneuver in the present environment. Now you are going to change the environment that made them successful. How you get the leaders to really support the change is a key question. What is in it for them to change?"

Smart drivers know
where traffic jams are before
they hit them. So do smart
change agents. Anticipate
problems and avoid them
before they arise.

The Project Patton plan for Kodak's war
against Big Ink and its emphasis on preparation inspired this
chapter, but its title comes from an IBM billboard I spotted more
recently: "Drivers can see traffic jams before they happen." I
wrote it down and sent it to Jim, my writer, with the note, "That's
exactly what change agents do."

Change agents can't avoid *all* problems, just as drivers can't
avoid all traffic. But we can prepare ourselves to anticipate those
problems and either avoid them, get around them, or attack them,
just as IBM did. (The ad said IBM "helped Singapore predict
traffic with 90% accuracy to anticipate and prevent congestion.")

Think about this in terms of car traffic. Whether you are driving down the 101 in Los Angeles, the L.I.E. in New York City, or
any road in Atlanta, you want to know where the problems are before you start. Sometimes you know because you've been down

that exact road before: you know where you are and where you want to go, what might and often does happen along the way, and what the solutions are or where to find them. But even if you are in a new city or another country, you know where you are and where you want to go; you just don't know what might happen and what the solutions are. Smart drivers find this out. They take the time to do their research. They listen and talk to people who have made this trip before to help them anticipate the traffic and normal intrusions that people who are unfamiliar with the terrain might not see. Before they begin, they ask this question: what could go wrong, and how have we prepared for that?

Actually that last question was number 18 in *The Mirror Test*'s list of 20 "win before you begin" questions I always ask when launching a marketing initiative (see Appendix A). And most change agents do this automatically after a while. We have learned to know what we don't know about where to go and what is coming up. Since we've dealt with the big attitude-adjustment issues and the roadblocks of our own (mood, people, and processes), we know to ask the question: where are the biggest jams going to be now? Forget about the competition for a second; just the lists of internal department jams can be huge: Legal, Internal, Sales, Finance, Marketing, Customer Service, IT . . .

Any big change initiative is not like a trip across town; it is like a cross-country trip. It is long and detailed, and you will need to make lots of decisions along the way. Still, you must stay focused on the big picture, which is probably why I love maps.

Yes, I still carry maps. I love holding a map in my hand and seeing everything that's in front of me—not just a tiny smartphone, tablet, or GPS screen that tells me where I am now. I want perspective. I want to see all the possibilities. When I go to a new city, I look at a map—a real map. When I go hunting, I study topography maps and detailed maps of the land to tell me where I'm supposed to go and what roads to take. I need to know what to do if I get hurt, and where help is if I am alone or if I am separated from my group. It's all about the preparation. When I give speeches, I map out the conversations I might have as a result of audience reaction or comments. When I go to meetings, I map out what will and might happen and what I need to say and do when it does. What exactly happens does not matter—that's details. The important part is I know things *will* happen, just as they will happen in any company and industry when driving changes that lead to growth, and my teams are prepared to deal with the details and get us there. The goal is the same: use all the tools you have to find the best path to reach your destination as quickly, efficiently, and directly as possible without losing time and depleting resources.

In other words, the point isn't to focus on how you turn left or exactly when you turn right. Remember: change agents don't want to explain or care about the process anymore—that's why we put those processes in place earlier in this book. I always say to my team, "I don't want a story. I get it." This is also why I take the time to develop teams I trust. I want my team to act like London cabdrivers—not because I want them to call me "Governor" when they greet me, but because London cabdrivers are the most trusted drivers in the world. You give them any destination, and they can get you there. Whatever address you give them, they know where it is and then think through the best ways of getting you there.

Don't believe me? Look it up. To get their licenses, drivers of official London hackney cabs have to study for a year *full time* to pass the test called "the Knowledge." This test requires them to know everything about getting around London, including where traffic jams are and when, how the traffic moves, and what the fastest routes are. They can't answer these questions with a GPS alone; they need maps and experience traveling the city, and then they need to commit it all to memory. London cabdrivers are so good at their job and have such a deep understanding of what they are doing that a study by the University of London has shown that their hippocampi—the part of the brain that handles spatial memory and navigation—are larger than those of the general public.

Given these facts, London cabdrivers may be the ultimate embodiment of George S. Patton's line, "Never tell people how to do things. Tell them what to do, and they will surprise you with their ingenuity." That's why, in Project Patton and Kodak's war with Big Ink, I was completely transparent about what was in front of us and what we needed in broad and specific detail. I told my team members to look at the "map" for perspective and understand all our opportunities and possibilities. I laid out our philosophy and the purpose of the group, the objectives and goals of the campaign, and processes and procedures like situation reports, metrics, and future agendas. I made sure they understood the three essential steps for competing:

- *Quantify and qualify.* Know how much business is at stake and that it is worth fighting for.

- *Compare.* Analyze and understand every aspect of the competition, from its production to its sales and marketing, with a clinical, unemotional eye.

- *Decide.* Plan to get ahead by building on your strengths and capitalizing on their weaknesses.

The members of my team also knew we would have ongoing progress meetings in our "situation room" with status updates on everything from sales and net realized rate (NRR) to other metrics. Finally, they knew we would always consider new actions to take in battling Big Ink.

That's a lot to prepare for, and again, that's why change agents spend so much time on internal processes early on (as I did with FAST at Kodak), *before* they start leading initiatives like these. In other words, I had trained my team members so they knew how to think big—they knew what to do—and I could trust them as we pushed to grow bigger. Every change agent lives for these fights and loves the challenges of growing bigger. As General Omar Bradley says to Patton in the movie *Patton*, "There's one big difference between you and me, George. I do this job because I've been trained to do it. You do it because you *love* it."

Chapter 21

The art of war: "Define your tactics to drive demand and translate potential combat power into victorious battles and engagements."

As George S. Patton said, no one should "fight a battle if you don't gain anything by winning." And winning in war and in business comes down to having strong tactics for your best-case and worst-case scenarios. Thus, your team members need to understand your *entire* tactical approach, your goals, and how you and they will be measured. To do that, you have to make sure they (and *you*) understand what *tactics* means.

When I was looking for a definition of the art of war to show the Big Ink Project Patton team, I turned to the *United States Army Field Manual 3-0*, which defines tactics as follows: "The ordered arrangement and maneuver of units in relation to each other and/or to the enemy in order to use their full potentialities. The employment of units in combat. It includes the ordered arrangement and maneuver of units in relation to each other, the terrain, and the enemy in order to *translate potential combat power into victorious battles and engagements*" [emphasis mine].

And if that's what is needed to win in war, I decided to educate my Project Patton team through a slide of actual military tactical maneuvers. Now, as I said before, I'm a son of the military; my father was in the military. I grew up on bases, and I played military when I was a kid. This tactical plan works for me, and it translates to business quite nicely when you want to understand the real definitions and meanings of tactics. Yeah, just as my cow-killing analogy made a few vegetarians go pale, this might upset a few doves, but any leader has got to see that the tactics I presented sound like business tactics as much as military ones. In fact, my team felt more empowered, capable, and resourceful when I laid out these tactics in Project Patton:

- Frontal attacks

- Breakthrough attempts and successful breakthroughs with stabilizing flanks and fortifications from rear operations

- Contra flanking with extended wings and mobile forces

- Hammer-and-anvil attacks with unyielding front anvils and mobile hammers

- Flank counterattacks

- Decoy and destruction attacks

- Full breakthrough attacks with an advance and preparation for counterattack

I explained all of these tactics with diagrams and actual battle examples. For example, I told my team about the Fetterman Massacre of 1866, when the Sioux, led by Crazy Horse, used a decoy strategy and had a small group of Indians pretend to be injured and lead the cavalrymen into a trap over the hills of the Big Horn Mountains. "The Sioux counterattacked an apparent breakthrough, approaching its competition from the side and winning," I told the team. "We need to think like this. We need to always think, 'What will we do, and then how will they respond?' If they do this, then we will need a breakthrough strategy and a hammer-and-anvil attack. If they do this, we will need to mount a counterattack."

I then connected these maneuvers to our pending war with Big Ink. Kodak knew a full frontal attack on the market was a bad idea (never approach a bull from the front!). There was no way we could go after the whole market. It was too large, and Big Ink was well established. So we decided to come in from the side and attract a more focused market segment: heavy users of inkjet printers. You weren't a heavy user? We did not want you. We wanted and needed people who used a lot of ink and would understand our value proposition of less expensive ink. Our goal, then, was "simple": to drive awareness of Kodak's revolutionary value proposition among ultra-high ink burners to drive consumer pull to retail and obtain a high net realized rate.

But to drive this value proposition, we needed to change the razor blade model Big Ink had created. The model now had to be that you pay a fair price for the printer, and then you get cheaper ink. We knew if we went after the heavy users, we could make a considerable amount of money even if we halved the price of the inkjet cartridges. We could move the product to higher margins and grow very effectively. Our sales and marketing tactics supported this goal by integrating our value proposition into a 360-degree global communications plan to reach our target consumer and deliver our message and value proposition in a compelling way. Our strategies included

- Expose the issues of Big Ink's model through the media and creative ads.

- Build momentum via paid media channels and publicity.

- Position all main competitors as Big Ink (which equals notorious decadence), as opposed to Kodak (which equals trust and value).

- Drive consumer pull.

As with all types of change, that was easier said than done. If we build it, will they come? Hardly. None of this guaranteed that the analysts, media, vendors, and consumers would buy into our new model. We still needed strong tactics, not only to sell our printers, but also to win over the point-of-sale people at big-box retailers first, educating them about Big Ink and the money they could make with our model. We had to stop them from consistently showing the "shiny mirror" and pushing Big Ink's virtually free printers to the consumer, but instead to drive the message that it was about the cost of the ink over and over and over again. They needed to know that our customers would keep buying and buying ink (and would usually pick up something else when they did). And we needed to stay top of mind by sending people into the stores to make sure the vendors were not defaulting to the shiny mirror model once we left. Only then would we have a chance to change the model and win.

Meanwhile, the production team was dealing with different tactical decisions, some of which would affect our tactics, such as whether our printers needed starter cartridges. Did Big Ink offer them? What's the use? Isn't including ink like giving the meat away? Should we tell people on the box if we include them? Should we tell people if we don't (like batteries not included)? Should we educate them that they need to buy ink, or is the idea that they will need it intuitive, like film used to be when you bought a camera? It sounds simple, but forgetting to question the simple things can really cost you in change. You can show all the super services and features that you have, but what if your customers say, "Hey, where's this thing we are used to?", never realize they needed to purchase ink, and can't get going when they unpack? You. Are. Screwed.

All of this is just some of how we created and applied our tactics in Project Patton, and why the gauntlet of change is not for the meek (especially if you're challenging a powerful sales model). It does not matter what industry you're in. If your quality is good, your message will stick—so stick to your guns.

In the end, it is always about selling what you have and not losing focus on where the money is made. And yet, even when you do all of this, that doesn't mean it all works the way you expected.

Chapter 22

Fail big! If you're going to fail with an idea, do it big, and then learn to take responsibility for what comes next.

Kodak's battle against Big Ink was progressing well on the business-to-business side. We were educating the key audiences and media about our goals and our financial results. We had compared our products' superior color capabilities and raised questions on technology capabilities with industry analysts. We were working closely with our vendors. We had solved the initial production problems. Now the question was, how do we portray Big Ink as being out of touch with our target customers? How do we capture those target customers' hearts and minds and make them *want* to engage us? Who would sell them on our story and make them act?

And that's when I had my big idea. Two words: Big Pussy. Not me, the character. We would hire Vinnie Pastore (Big Pussy) of *The Sopranos* and create a spot trading on the continued appeal of the show to highlight Kodak's inkjet printer's value proposition.

The spot begins with Vinnie parking his car by what looks to be the Jersey docks. He looks angry as he opens the trunk. Whoever is in that trunk is going to get whacked. "I've been waiting a long time for this," he frowns. "All the pain and suffering, bleeding me dry for years. You had to be greedy, didn't you? You kept taking and taking."

Then we see what—not who—has made Vinnie so angry: a printer. "You gave me nothing! Cheating me, far too long!" he scowls, taking the printer out of the car. "You sucked me in with your low printer prices, and then stabbed me in the back with ridiculous, high ink prices!" He sets the printer on the ground and smashes it to pieces with a baseball bat, yelling, "You deceived the family. Now you get what you deserve!"

Vinnie then gets back in the car, and next to him is a Kodak inkjet printer. He pats it and says, "Welcome to the family." The message: "Don't get whacked by high inkjet prices. Text us and we'll send you a coupon."

As we got the spot ready, we started building a campaign around this value proposition to engage consumers instantly. This was all happening before the meteoric rise of Facebook and the launch of Twitter, but after people were voting with their thumbs for contestants on *American Idol* and other reality shows. And BlackBerries were everywhere for e-mail. So, I decided on a mobile texting and e-mail campaign. We would play the spot in movie theaters to a captive audience. Consumers would text or e-mail us if they hated Big Ink, and we would send them electronic discount coupons for our high-quality, value-priced printers and ink.

This was what marketers dream of: a slam dunk. The idea and execution were clever and funny, *and* on message. And I'm not just saying that. In tests, not only was it universally loved, but it also got double-digit responses. Double-digit is huge. Heck, marketers know high-single-digit is great, and even low-single-digit is sometimes fine. But double-digit? We were stoked.

I told the team to go and start the rollout in Chicago, buying time on screens in every single movie theater on the coming big release weekend.

That weekend, I wondered, "How many responses could there be? Thousands? Hundreds of thousands? A million?"

I rolled in on Monday ready for the results and all the coupons we sent out. The team came in and put a sheet of paper in front of me with the number of texts: 2.

"Two million!?" No, just two.

"Two hundred thousand?" No, two.

"Two hundred . . . twenty . . . ?"

Two.

Two. We had gone out on a limb. We had put ourselves in front of millions of people. We had a clever and creative campaign that couldn't lose. And we got two texts to show for it.

"Will somebody please explain to me what happened here? We had double-digit responses! Double. Digit. Responses. It was funny. Even HP would agree. It was on message. Can somebody please explain to me what went wrong?"

Clearly, we had failed. I looked at the team. The team knew it.

Then someone from the back said, "Jeff, what's the first thing you are asked to do when you walk into a movie theater?"

Turn off your phones. They couldn't text us because their phones were off (or they had forgotten they were on), and who remembers to do something like this *after* the movie?

"Where the hell were you when we came up with this idea?" I said.

At this point in most stories, too many leaders want to find someone to blame or share the responsibility for failing. And I admit the temptation to deflect accountability can be strong. But change agents accept the fact that failure is inevitable sometimes, especially when you think big. (The best home run hitters in baseball know that swinging for the fences means you will also strike out, usually a lot.) It's how you act and what you do next that matters: you must take responsibility and hold yourself accountable at all points.

I took a deep breath and took responsibility. "Okay, guys, this sucks," I told them. "This is my fault, but while we failed, no one is going to die. Hey, we failed in the best possible way: we failed big. If you're going to fail, do it big! So, what's next? We still have a great spot and a great idea. Let's repurpose it and redo it, and let's learn a lesson on how to act, together."

Our FAST organizing principles came into play here, too. We had not achieved our goals, but I was holding myself accountable for the achievement of those goals. We had screwed up, but we had done it FAST-er! And if speed is good, but FAST is better, it was time for even FAST-er solutions. I then walked through what we were going to do: putting the spot on our internal and public websites, posting it on YouTube, adding links to it in our company e-mails, and giving it to our sales force to use as an opening for presentations. The spot would never work the way we intended, but now the team knew that failing and failure are not the same.

Be prepared to attack, respond, and *not* respond. Decide what you're going to defend and what you're going to let go.

During the first years of Kodak's inkjet initiative, Big Ink did not attack us. It mostly ignored us, like a gnat flying around its competitive bull. Its approach seemed to be to pay no attention to us and hope that we went away. But small is small only if you are not thinking big, and we had big ideas—and soon we had big results to match.

In Kodak's first two years battling Big Ink and targeting high-volume inkjet printer users, the company generated gains of 300 to 400 percent. Then again, when you start from zero, you'd better show those kinds of gains! Big Ink could have crushed us then and there, but it laughed us off—not a bad approach as long as you keep paying attention. By the third year, Kodak was seeing gains of 150 percent, and our profitability projections were moved up by as much as a year given the volume we were doing. Our niche market approach had made Kodak's initial millions in revenue small in comparison to Big Ink's billions in profits, but now we were growing by hundreds of millions a year. Our printers had started at number seven in most categories, but now we had leapt into the top three in most categories. Our target audience indeed consumed twice as many inkjet cartridges as regular users, and we were winning over their hearts and minds.

But when would Big Ink respond? Change agents know you can pick a fight, but it is only when your target fights back that you know it is paying attention and you are more than just a blip on its radar screen. We welcome attacks as much as we welcome compliments and comments. We love them—as change agents, we need them! Because we don't pick fights we think we will lose. We needed Big Ink to respond, so we repeatedly poked it with our results and our deliberately offensive-minded campaigns. We wanted Big Ink to take a swing at us. And finally it did.

Big Ink's response was full-throated and pretty nasty, but we were ready for it. When you are as tactically prepared as we were and the competition is slow to fight back, you have time to prepare to respond. And you can win a fight playing your game if you follow a similar approach to our philosophy with Big Ink in battle (and my philosophy in general): attack on most things—move with shock and awe.

In war, Patton believed attacking saved lives, that an ounce of sweat could save a gallon of blood. In the war against Big Ink, Project Patton believed attacking made money, that an ounce of sweat could make us a lot of money. Both ideas require pushing your "company" to stay on top of every single counterattack and offensive. And if you're starting a business battle that's as full-scale as Kodak's with Big Ink (many targets, different approaches, varied tactics), you'll also need to create separate teams to defend each of the moving parts. These teams will allow you to open "flanks" on competitive "fronts" (for example, business-to-consumer and business-to-business) so you don't lose focus on your enemy/competition. In Project Patton, I actually had people responsible for "war team coordination" and then organized the rest of my marketing people into teams that covered areas like

- Opposition research

- Online advertising

- Social networking

- Customer care

- Retailer tools and efforts

- Kodak employee effort

- Press, analysts, bloggers

The goal for the captains who led each of these teams was to get and keep the inkjet trust and value high ground smartly and quickly. (They also worked extra carefully to keep everything we did secret from the competition; we had leaks, and in the age of social media, *everyone* can get leaked information instantly.) Each team picked its opportunities and decided how to attack and what it would defend. And the teams were able to do this FAST and make decisions more quickly and better than ever before with the process and tactical training they already had.

We exploited public market share data to show that our gains meant Big Ink had slipped—no matter how the data portrayed the size of our business, that meant we were winning. We got to rating and review sites with an active campaign to tout our printers' quality and ink value proposition. We pushed hard to make our vendors aware of what we offered. We smothered Kodak customers with attention and treated anyone who was experiencing issues with extraordinary care, turning those potential problems into opportunities.

We used our ongoing oppositional research to attack quickly, pointing out the differences between our model and the Big Ink model. We hit it with "green" research. When Big Ink posted websites loaded with derogatory pages full of misleading information about our printers, we had BigInkFacts.com ready to counter this misleading info and simply say "for shame" for being so nasty. Big Ink started taking down its sites.

But then there were the roads not taken. Sometimes you don't need to defend yourself, no matter how withering the assault. If you're going to attack someone or something, you've got to be prepared for your target to respond. And that's when you need to be prepared *not to respond*. You have to decide what you're going to defend and what you're going to let go and stop reacting in a vacuum to every bad word, piece of news, result, and day, taking them too seriously and getting defensive.

I learned a lot from my CEOs at Kodak and Cenveo about how to do this. When you lead a public company or a business that's in the public eye, people will come after you publicly, and both these CEOs showed great restraint and strength in the face of often withering criticism. They stayed aware of what was going on and who, where, and how people were saying what and why. But then they ignored most of it.

To handle it all, you sometimes do some extra messaging with and show kindness to your troops to keep their morale up and hold steady. Sometimes it means just saying "for shame" and learning to turn the other cheek and stay positive and on message when the media or others try to bait you into going negative. You can even enlist the help of your customers or your audience. When Kodak hosted a Twitter conversation about our inkjet printers, Big Ink joined in but did not disclose its affiliation, trying to hijack the conversation in the most disingenuous way: hiding its true reason for being on Twitter. This "person" then proceeded to bad-mouth our printer. Did we respond? No. We held our tongue, and the Twitter community did our work for us: its members searched for the person's true identity, found that he worked for Big Ink, and exposed his bias and dishonesty in not disclosing those ties. They requested that the person apologize and say something nice or move on. He finally moved on, that twanker. (Twanker is my term for a person, organization, or company who uses bad form or exhibits bad behavior on Twitter. You can find all my names for people who sometimes make Twitter suck in *The Mirror Test.*)

At Kodak, we even took imitation as the highest form of flattery. I nearly peed in my pants when a Big Ink company took Kodak's inkblot ad and turned it into its own. But that's pretty much all I did. Imitation is going to happen when you take the high ground, so get over it. And in this case, as in most cases of imitation, many people thought it was our ad, anyway. Thanks, Big Ink!

Chapter 24

Nothing personal? Of course it is! But don't take the bait. Don't believe the bad stuff. Grow a thicker skin and take the high road.

VIVIAN: People put you down enough you start to believe it.

EDWARD: I think you are a very bright, very special woman.

VIVIAN: The bad stuff is easier to believe. You ever notice that?

Vivian (Julia Roberts), the hooker with a heart of gold in *Pretty Woman*, had it right. It *is* always easier to believe the bad stuff. And boy is there a lot of bad stuff out there: a blog and 140 characters are all you need these days to attack people or companies and cut them off at the knees. You don't even need to show your name, let alone your face. This is why the ability to *not* respond goes for personal attacks, too. I'm not talking about responding to legitimate complaints customers have about your product or services. (Later I'll talk about radical transparency and engaging customer problems.) I'm talking about *you*.

When I appeared on *Celebrity Apprentice* for Kodak, online comments said I had a "face for radio" and asked if my wife wanted a recommendation for a personal trainer for me (nothing about the content of what I said). When I published *The Mirror Test*, an Amazon "reviewer" proudly stated he had "not read the book," but had no problem giving it one star, posted negative anonymous quotes about me from supposed Kodak employees, and said I was an "ego-maniac" who wears "ugly suits."

Did I respond to any of these? No. I wasn't even a big enough egomaniac to tell the Amazon guy that the word is not spelled with a hyphen. (Well, until now.) What was I going to do? Believe everything would be better if I just went on a diet and bought a different suit? I laugh the bad stuff off, and so should you. The bad stuff is easy and even fun to dish out and react to. Good stuff just doesn't make for good stories or excuses.

Change agents are always going to hear more negative than positive comments even when they succeed—or perhaps especially when they succeed. (Pauline Kael, the former film critic for the *New Yorker*, was once asked how she felt about everyone either loving her or hating her. Her answer? "That means everyone is reading me!") We need to remain thick-skinned and unemotional, and ignore the critics—even more so when we are confronted directly. Remember Dale Carnegie's words: "Any fool can criticize, condemn, and complain—and most fools do." (And if you do respond, at least remember you should never criticize people until you have walked a mile in their shoes; that way you're a mile away from them and you have their shoes.)

Of course, e-mail and social media have just made the bad stuff travel faster and be harder to avoid. I can't tell you how many times I have gotten emotional, personally insulting, and mean notes that ripped me a new one for something I supposedly did or said. Folks tell me I am responsible for everything bad that happened to them, their friends and family, and my company, and thus by abstraction my family, my hometown, every business I worked for, the government, and indeed the world.

But change agents are used to this. As I said before, they are the white buffaloes of decision making. So what if these personal attacks are leveled at you as a corporate representative? Do you engage then? Sometimes. Sometimes you need to fight aggressively but not publicly.

At one point, one of Big Ink's bloggers came after me personally on Twitter—not my performance or the company, but *me*. Bad form. But after a few news outlets, including the *Wall Street Journal*, picked up the criticism, I got on the phone and called the Big Ink executive in charge of the campaign, who happened to be a friend. I told him this was a really piss-poor way of leading the battle. "There's no reason to make this personal," I told him. "In fact, keep this up and I can't wait to say publicly that I'm not surprised about this coming from a company that wiretapped its own board of directors. How'd you like to see that on the front page of the *Wall Street Journal*?"

In this case, I did not choose to respond to this attack because I wanted to defend my own integrity. I did it because I wanted Big Ink to come after my company—not me. I could not care less if it came after me. People come after me all the time, but when the *Wall Street Journal* gets involved? Now it's more than a small nuisance; it's distracting from the point of the campaign. That was the purpose of my phone call—not to make threats or protect myself, but to get the focus *off of me* and back on our story. I needed the focus on the story we wanted. I wanted Big Ink to challenge Kodak's model. I wanted it to talk about the ink. I wanted to lure Big Ink into our channel where we could ambush it. That's how I wanted it to respond—that was my single-minded focus. Heck, if the attack on me had benefited Kodak? Well, then, go ahead: attack away! But it didn't, so I dealt with it way beyond the public eye.

This is hard to do when everything these days is in the public eye and the gauntlet of criticism can be painful. When Kodak launched the Kodak Challenge with the PGA Tour, someone wrote the local newspaper that this was my way of getting to play golf with all my buddies. In this case, the info was so insider we knew it had to be one of our employees (guard those leaks!) who was pissed off about how and where Kodak was spending its money and on what divisions. Never mind that our CEO was the one who gave this program the green light and how hurtful it was to him to see that article in his hometown paper. Never mind that I actually was not the one who came up with this brilliant promotional idea. Let's just focus for a moment instead on the fact that I don't like golf. Will I play it? Sure. Do I watch it on TV? Sometimes. But I'd rather drive the beverage cart on a course than play. I'm a hunter and a cowboy, not a golfer. My clubs were bought at a garage sale 15 years ago. Yet I'm getting criticized because that was all I wanted to do? In fact, when we made the decision to go with the PGA Tour and the Kodak Challenge, I was grateful for the excuse *not* to play, because it would have been a conflict of interest. My best response in this case was to let my actions speak for themselves. I never played a round of golf at Kodak after that.

In the end, your integrity is best preserved by not engaging with personal attacks made by dishonest, inauthentic cowards who comment anonymously and would not dare to say anything to your face. My sincere hope is that you have nothing to apologize for because you never responded the first time and took the high road even when you were given the opening to go low. Instead, beat 'em the best way possible: with success! They'll just disappear, even if their words live on in cyberspace. Occasionally, they do get back in touch to apologize for what they said!

One time I got an e-mail that basically placed me north of Benedict Arnold and just south of Adolf Hitler on the evil scale for all the damage I had done at Kodak. Since the writer had contacted me directly from a legitimate e-mail address, I e-mailed him back to acknowledge I had received his note and suggested he check out some information that might paint me in a different light. Here's the start of an actual e-mail I received in response:

> Mr. Hayzlett, I can be a jerk at times, and the wonderful invention of e-mail only exacerbates my occasional crime. Last night I read the e-mail you sent me; did a cursory web search on you, had in my mind memories of friends in Rochester who worked at Kodak and were laid off during the time you were there, and I came to the most brilliant conclusion that their layoffs must have been your fault! And then, in an emotional state, I wrote you back—a stupid, brainless and insulting e-mail—for which I sincerely apologize.
>
> I am sending this e-mail because I wanted to publicly (in front of the folks on this e-mail) apologize to you, but also because I have done some additional exploration of the facts.

He went on for a few screen lengths, citing the work he had done in researching my character, and ended by hoping I would accept his apology. In response, I simply said this:

> Thank you for this note. Appreciate the gesture. As you get to know me, one of my favorite sayings is, "no one died!" Certainly the case here. My wife reacted much the same way when we first met, and we are still together 30 years later— so there is a lot of hope for us! Let's make something good of this all.

Chapter 25

Make it personal! Get as close to your customers as you possibly can, and then get closer still so you can give them a squeeze.

I was standing at the printer bar at Best Buy when the customer approached me.

"Hey, I saw you on TV this week. The Kodak guy, right? Wow. You get fired?"

What I'm wanted to say was, "Yes, that's what happened. I'm knee-deep in Kodak's growing war against Big Ink, and I just generated millions of dollars of national broadcast exposure for Kodak on *Celebrity Apprentice*—so Kodak just up and said, 'You're fired!'" And then wink. But I couldn't risk a joke like that falling flat or, worse, being taken seriously. This wasn't about me.

So what I said was, "No, I just work here nights. I love our printers, cameras, and customers so much, I just can't help myself."

This kind of encounter was happening more and more at Best Buy, Staples, and OfficeMax stores (mostly near Rochester, New York, and Sioux Falls, South Dakota—my home bases during my

Kodak years). It's not so easy being undercover when you've been on network prime time. Not that I was really trying to go undercover. Besides, I'm 6'3" tall and 270 pounds. Who are you going to disguise me as?

I was at Best Buy that day to connect with our vendors and customers and sell for Kodak—just as I have for every company I have ever owned, worked for, or represented. (I did this so much in the Rochester and Sioux Falls areas that most of the sales staff said, "Hi, Jeff!" when I walked in the door.) I always say, "Sell yourself, sell the company!" and if my appearances on national TV or any other promotional appearances helped me do that for Kodak, I was happy to be recognized.

In fact, the only thing I wanted to be "secret" about my store visits was when I showed up. Unless I am doing a scheduled presentation or event, that's exactly how I want it to be: an everyday experience. I wanted to see what our products and our competitors looked like from the customers' point of view and hear how they were being presented by the vendors; then sometimes stay and present them myself! On this day, I was there because Kodak needed to make sure the salespeople at our vendors were not ignoring our printers and showing the "shiny mirror" of Big Ink's virtually free printers to their customers. I was there to drive our value proposition home.

Sure, we had secret shoppers doing this, too. We also had research to tell us how it was going on the numbers side. And yeah, our salespeople checked in all the time. But does that tell you first-hand what your vendors are doing and how it looks from the customer's perspective and without your employees' filter?

I did this every day I possibly could while I worked for Kodak—not just during the Big Ink days. It's lunchtime; I'm driving over to a store. When I'm in a city, there's a Best Buy; I'm going in. There's a Staples; I'm going in. There's an OfficeMax; I'm going in. I *have* to see what that is like. Why wouldn't you want to do this? What makes anyone at any company, *especially* change agents, think this is beneath them or not their job? This is walking the talk of customer service: experiencing for yourself what the customers and frontline people experience.

I went into stores hundreds and hundreds of times, introduced myself to the staff, and then helped them sell cameras over my competitors, standing by the printer or camera bar and engaging our customers directly. I didn't want to plan a visit, but this was no sneak attack. "Hi, I'm Jeff Hayzlett, the chief marketing officer from Kodak, and I'm so excited by this product of ours that I'm standing here selling it to you in Omaha." No one deserves to have an inferior sale experience—not the customer and not my product.

Change agents and everyone at a company from top to bottom should be encouraged to do this with their vendors and their customers in order to understand the front lines of their businesses from the sales and service side. You can do it up front or you can go undercover, but either way: do it!

If you have any doubt this is a powerful idea that resonates with most people, look at the show CBS gave the lucrative, highly coveted, hugely hyped post–Super Bowl 2010 spot on its schedule to: *Undercover Boss*. The show follows chief executives from companies like 7-Eleven, Hooters, and White Castle as they slip anonymously into the rank and file of their companies to see how they are really working. Larry O'Donnell, CEO of Waste Management, starred in the Super Bowl episode. Larry O'Donnell is a real stand-up guy, but could he stand up to the everyday demands of trash pickup? The answer was no. O'Donnell not only performed the work poorly, but also chafed under some of the rules his managers enforced—rules he had ostensibly put into place as CEO!

He was fired from his undercover job.

O'Donnell then revealed himself to his employees, told them what he had learned, and changed the rules he had found so onerous. His employees applauded and hugged him.

He not only got close enough to give his people a hug, but also got one! It was great TV.

What are you doing to find out more about how you serve your customers and what it takes for your people to handle your customers? Even if hugging is not your thing, you can reap the other benefits from being an undercover boss at your company, no television production required. Stop relying on "How am I doing?" cards and surveys no one ever cares about. Open your and *all* your employees' eyes to everything that is happening on the front lines of service by getting out there:

- Walk into stores.

- Visit with your customers and vendors.

- Call in orders or have your friends do it and listen.

- Work the front desk.

- Dial into customer service, know when you get good service and when you don't, and acknowledge it.

- Have your managers and executives take complaint calls.

- Review the online chatter on web and social media sites (more on this in a bit).

We all pay lip service to the idea of customer relationships. *We need to believe it.* Change agents need to make sure everyone at their company treats its customers and the people who connect with it better than they treat themselves. Customers are the lifeblood of any business, and they can come and go as they please. Building relationships with them is a bond that is almost like family—they'll stick with you as long as you don't lie, cheat, or try to pull the wool over their eyes.

I know your next question: can you measure this in your bottom line? Sometimes. But most of it comes back to something I said in *The Mirror Test*: quality leads to impact. You may not be able to measure all this in specific hard numbers, but in an age when feedback can happen at any time from any device, the dividends always offset a different ROI: return on ignoring.

At Kodak, we cultivated this kind of culture when we went back to George Eastman's principles of customer service. And I like to think he would have been delighted to know my salespeople and I were not the only people who headed into the stores while we battled Big Ink. We had customers out there too, happy to help us out . . . evangelizing, tweeting, and texting to tell us what was going on.

Friendsourcing My Gravy-Sucking Pig Caveat

As you know from *The Mirror Test*, I am not above turning the tables and firing customers, especially the "gravy-sucking pigs"—those customers who suck up everything at the "trough" of your business (far more than their fair share) and are still never satisfied. These customers and any like them should and must be put to slaughter as soon as possible. These customers distract you from the customers who need your attention and drive your bottom line! Sure, some of these customers turn out to be gravy-sucking pigs, or what my friend Pete Deutschman of the Buddy Group called in Chapter 9 "skunks," only after they are gone. But they never were on the good side of your business's Pareto principle, the law of the vital few, most commonly called the "80-20 rule," which states that 80 percent of your business comes from 20 percent of your clients.

And you can do this in *any* business. Ann M. Devine is executive director of Pi Sigma Epsilon, a not-for-profit that reports to a board of directors—a board that at one point was totally dysfunctional. I actually consulted with Ann to replace existing board members with strong new leadership; she just initially forgot to show patience and kindness during the process: "I sucked at doing it. I pissed off a couple of people on the board and went head-to-head with our awards chair. I was a bull in a china shop and refused to wait it out a bit longer. I forgot my number one rule to '*Always* allow other people to save face.' I lost my temper with her, and, as a result, some others went with her. They needed to leave anyway, as they were inhibiting change, but I could have done it differently."

Chapter 26

Do your customer service George Eastman style: "You press the button, we do the rest." Next time, ask yourself, "What would George do?"

"You press the button, we do the rest."

"We were starting out to make photography an everyday affair, to make the camera as convenient as the pencil."

"The Kodak Camera makes possible a collection of photographs which record the life of its owner and which increase in value each day that passes."

These are three of my favorite lines from George Eastman, founder of the Eastman Kodak Company. A self-educated high school dropout, Eastman used his entrepreneurial spirit, wonderful imagination, and flair for both innovation and organization to turn Kodak into a great American brand. Whether Kodak is relevant to your life anymore, its power as a brand was and in many ways still is undeniable. Even for consumers today: people who don't even know what a roll of film looks like use the term *Kodak Moment* to describe a moment when something special happened in their lives—whether they took a picture of it or not.

Similarly, those lines from Eastman are utterly relevant to any business today. Not what he is talking about (film and cameras), but what he wanted Kodak to do: serve the customer, make it easy, and get close—real close (enhance those customer bonds). They should be the service motto of the change agent, and they became mine in Kodak's battle with Big Ink and every initiative I launched.

Not that I knew any of this about Eastman when I joined Kodak and took over as CMO. I knew Kodak. I knew our business. But one Saturday I found myself sitting alone in my office, looking out the window, and wondering if I had Eastman's office or even where his office was. That's when I realized I didn't know enough about him.

I went down to his grave at Kodak Park to visit his memorial. I then (of course) started to clean up around his grave and the eternal flame that burns there. The security guards were about to shoo me away before they realized who I was.

"Jeff Hayzlett? What are *you* doing here?"

"Trying to remember and get back to who we are and what we are trying to do."

Next, I raided the archives and started reading everything Eastman had written—correspondence, internal memos, ads he had designed (he wrote the copy, too). What I discovered was that George Eastman was a change agent not only in industry, but also inside his business! He had one of the first female executive secretaries when all of the others in the 1880s were male. In fact, he put women in the workforce like no one else did (he did let them go an hour early so they could make dinner for their families). His ads were cutting-edge, even racy. I was getting crap for pushing too much, but Eastman pushed farther than I ever could.

But Eastman never pushed if he felt the push violated one of his three tenets: serve the customer, make it easy, and get close—

real close. That was the emotional connection Kodak had with its customers for more than a century. I told everyone at the company that *all* our customer relations—the serving and servicing of our customers—had to be about these three things. That was what we were going to drive through everything we did, and then we would make sure our customers knew about it.

I realized that these three things were the answer to the question, "What would George do?" I realized they were the very foundation of what we were and always had been as a company. Kodak would fail if the changes took it away from the core of what it is as a company. So, we started by asking our customers what they wanted and incorporating the feedback into our products. For example, we asked, "How do we make our digital cameras as easy to use as a pencil? Is it design? Is it enhancements? Is it price?" (In that case, we discovered that 90 percent of all people use the default button on the camera, so we put all the top 10 features that people wanted, such as facial recognition and red-eye reduction, into the default.)

Are you doing this in your business? Before specialization, before marketing, before anything . . . are you continually focused on service? And if so, how can you do it *better*? Just because we are more *connected* than ever—just because social media makes everyone a tweet away—doesn't mean a *connection* is being made. Your presence must be felt, not just heard.

What would George do? Serve the customer, make it easy, and get close—real close. Don't just say it, do it.

Friendsourcing Caring for Customers

Customers don't and won't care about you until you deliver and keep your brand promise to them, and that requires you to do one thing first: care about them. That's why I was in those Best Buys. That's why I spend so much time creating programs that directly connect to my customers. Great change agents know they *need* to do this, and to do it the way our customers want it, not just the way we want to do it. As George Eastman knew, there's more value if you do it the way they want it. My friend Ray Tom echoes this when he "strives to give excellent customer service, which incorporates the focus of making your customer's job easier." So does Ronald M. Turner, CME, president of We Care/HydroMaid, who knows, "The best decisions are made after you look at the problem or program from the customer's point of view."

But no one understands this more than Dr. Nido Qubein, president of High Point University and chairman of Great Harvest Bread Co. Nido is one of the great speakers and storytellers I know, and his "holistic" approach to capturing and transforming the families and students at High Point sums up what caring for customers can do:

> At High Point University, when we began treating families as customers (something most universities do not do), we began to see transformational change and have seen amazing growth in our student enrollment and retention as a result. We paid special attention to the student experience by emphasizing a holistic educational experience. At every turn, we model life values to students so that parents understand and appreciate the distinctive learning environment that we offer and "every student receives an extraordinary education in an inspiring environment with caring people." For me, the inspiration to do this comes immediately from the smile of a student or a note from a graduate about their experience at HPU. At HPU, we are inspired every day to continue our work because we know it makes a difference in the lives of young people who go on to achieve great things and effect meaningful change for the better in our world.

Chapter 27

Speed means nothing if your customers only get annoyed faster. Don't just *say* customer service is a priority—make it one.

My friend Dr. Tracy Smith loved a software program he had been using for work, but he needed an upgrade to something more powerful. He had been completely satisfied with the older version of the software, so he decided to try that company's new version first. He downloaded a trial upgrade, good for 30 days, and liked it. When he got the message "Trial over, you need to purchase the full working version," he did what many of us do every day: he went to the site, entered his credit card information, and chose the "instant download" option.

Tracy didn't want to wait for a disk. He wanted instant productivity and gratification, and he had chosen the option that got him that. Or so he thought. After purchasing his "instant download," Tracy got a message telling him he would receive e-mail confirmation of his order and that "once manual authorization is approved," he would "receive further instructions in the next business day."

What? Tracy wasn't purchasing anything expensive or illicit. His credit card was paid up, and he had never had a problem using it. Why could he not instantly download the product he had just paid to instantly download? Further instructions? What was this, *Mission Impossible*?

Note: this was not something from some start-up; it was a well-known product from a leading software company that has software on almost every computer today. Since Tracy liked and wanted the software, he was angry, but he was not a lost customer . . . yet. He believed this was a simple mistake and that he just needed to talk to someone to get it resolved.

But Tracy also knew what many of us already know or are learning every day: 800 numbers and their endless and frustrating menus are lost causes, especially after hours. In fact, 800 numbers are going the way of the dinosaur in the age of online chats, Twitter, and texts. Yet survey after survey shows that customers prefer instant service *and* a human touch (see this chapter's friendsourcing sidebar). That's what Tracy wanted: to get some instant service, an explanation, and resolution of his instant download problem. He clicked to request a customer service online chat and logged his reason as "problem with instant download." The following is the transcript of the "chat" that Tracy had with the customer service representative. Only the name of the rep has been changed.

REP: Hello! Welcome to _____ Customer Service.

REP: Hi Tracy.

REP: Could you please be more specific on your concern?

TRACY: Why can't I download my purchase I just made?

TRACY: It says "reviewing your order," and I'll receive information in 1 business day. Ridiculous.

TRACY: Order #_____

REP: Let me check and help you with this.

REP: Tracy, I checked and see that this order is held for manual authorization and you'll get a reply via e-mail once the order is processed.

TRACY: I don't want to wait. I am working with the product now ... why do I have to wait? I provided credit card information.

TRACY: I downloaded the upgrade "trial version" and if I can't work with it now, I will just cancel my order and download something else.

REP: Tracy, I am sorry for this inconvenience, when the order is held for manual authorization we have no option to release it until it falls from manual authorization.

TRACY: I think this policy is absurd. I have never purchased something online only to have to wait for "manual authorization." Is there a supervisor that can help me?

TRACY: Can it be manually authorized now?

TRACY: I am working with the product for work purposes, but cannot continue until I download the full working version, which I just submitted credit information to pay for.

TRACY: Now I'm being told to wait.

REP: Thank you for waiting. One moment please.

REP: Sorry for the wait. Please do stay online.

REP: I'll be right with you.

REP: Tracy, I am really sorry for this inconvenience, since the order is held for manual authorization we have no option to release it until it falls out from the manual authorization.

REP: Sorry for the wait. Please do stay online.

TRACY: What in the world is a "manual authorization" anyway? Do you have the almighty wizard locked up in a room pressing the "authorization" button so I can finally have the product I paid for online? LOL

TRACY: This is great. Actually I'm not even mad now, I'm laughing at this policy.

REP: Tracy, normally it takes 2 business days to process your order once you place the order online.

REP: And since this order is placed on Jan. 13, 2011, 8:18:40 PM PST, I request you to wait until the order get [sic] processed and you'll receive an e-mail notification once the order is processed.

TRACY: Well, that might make sense if I was drunk. It's an online purchase to download. Not wait. If I wanted to wait, I wouldn't have checked the "instant download" button to buy. There isn't a disclaimer telling me I have to wait.

TRACY: I will not purchase from your company again.

TRACY: Rep, none of this is personal. I know you are just working. But please, pass this up the chain. Good night.

Tracy proceeded to cancel his order and download (instantly) another company's software, which worked just fine. He refuses to buy anything from the other company again. Lost customer. Lost evangelist for the product. Lost opportunity.

What I love (and hate) about Tracy's experience is that it is completely unexceptional. It reads like a transcript of a call we have all had with 800-number operators. Come on—no way you didn't feel Tracy's frustration or sided with the rep. Even when he got testy, he was not insulting and was apologetic in a completely exasperated but genuine way. On the other hand, the apologies from the customer service rep seemed rote and fueled Tracy's indignation. Unfortunately, as I said, this is unexceptional.

So, what's the exceptional version of this? My experience and the experience of people I asked shows that good online service starts the same way it does in person: not with an apology for the problem, but with awareness *that there is in fact a problem* to begin with. We all enjoy it when reps are personable and reflect the personality of the company, but that matters less than whether they just *solve our problems*.

No one logs into customer service chats to sing a company's praises. Maybe she just wants to place an order and can't figure something out. Maybe he is deciding whether or not to order the product or service and is having trouble finding the information he needs in order to make that decision. Maybe he has a problem with a product or a service he received or ordered. Maybe there's a billing question or problem. Maybe she can't get the product or service she wants or is canceling a product or service.

Whatever it is, the customer has a problem, and the rep needs to be aware of it and solve it—fast. If a rep can't solve the problem immediately, there are two options: emphasize that this is ridiculous or unusual and "pass it up the chain," as Tracy suggested, or investigate and get back in touch with the customer immediately. Need more evidence than Tracy's account that this is a problem? In its 2011 national survey on customer service, *Consumer Reports* ("What's Wrong with Customer Service," July 2011, pp. 16–18) found that people still wanted to talk to a human to deal with service issues.

- The survey found that 71 percent of respondents were "tremendously annoyed" when they couldn't reach a human on the phone, and 56 percent felt that way about having to take multiple phone steps to reach the right place.

Not surprising, right? These days, instant service on the phone seems to happen only when you call a local or small business, which is a real competitive advantage for those businesses—if you are one, don't screw it up! I mean, what resident from what circle of hell designed those endless phone trees and passed them off as a good idea for customer service? Here's a hint: if you make people press 20 buttons to get to a human, you're gonna piss them off. According to the same *Consumer Reports* study, people are even willing to wait for attention on the phone as long as they get great service when they do. The problem is, they don't:

- According to the survey, 67 percent hung up the phone without having their problem solved, and 64 percent said that they had left a store because service was poor.

Come on, people, do we need to remind you of the basics? Customers care about how you respond and treat them before, during, and *after* the sale. Sure, customers who eat at a buffet can't expect to get great service, too. We all love getting a great deal at a big-box store, but we often pay for it again when there is a problem. Customers need to understand that, just like diners at a restaurant, if they want service on a real plate at a table, they have to pay for it. They are paying for that ongoing attention. And if they have paid for it, you'd better give it to them. Again, smaller businesses have an advantage here—don't screw it up!

But ultimately it comes down to this: if you care about what you sell and service, customers will care about you. Remember what I said before: information can be delivered and feedback can happen from any device in an instant these days. This is ground zero for improving instant feedback. It is part of a different ROI I talk about: the return on ignoring. The higher the quality of your service, the more impact you will have, so make it exceptional.

Again, leaders must do what they need to do in order to understand what their customers are experiencing and stay on top of *all* their customer service "fronts" by going undercover. Make inquiries and ask questions on the phone, in person, on e-mail, in chats, and via text requests. Order your products online and intentionally order the wrong product or service. Order it to arrive in different ways. Then, try to exchange or cancel or get credit for it. Use a chat or social media to try to resolve your problem. In different chats, be difficult, nice, confused, or angry—take notes and save the transcripts.

And make it real—*real* orders with an eye on what works and what needs to change. Address the problems. Repeat.

Friendsourcing Listening

Customer service is all about capturing and listening to your customers, and the phone and certainly social media can't replace the human touch. People are not particularly adept at listening on social media—*really* listening. We tend to talk *at* each other when we chat, text, tweet, and post. E-mail for a conversation? That's no better than a smoke signal these days—it's great for saying yes or no and passing along information, but beyond that, its utility goes way down. In the age of Skype, there's no reason not to have a face-to-face conversation, but even that's only one tool.

And even when you have the human touch, you need to *want* to listen to those customers.

That's what Dina Kaplan, cofounder of blip.tv, found out the hard way: "We got thrown from the saddle right when we launched the company, because we hadn't spent enough time listening to our customers and really engaging the thought leaders in our community. The month that we started, they didn't pay attention to us at all, and we almost shut the company down. Over the following few months, only by pinpointing and engaging a few really influential people in our industry and listening to them did they have enough trust in us to try our product and eventually to recommend it to many people in their worlds."

Clark Kokich, chairman of Razorfish, discovered something similar when there was a management change at his biggest client: "We had done a great job for them, and were confident we were on the right track. As a result, we failed to listen to where the new team was going. We said we were being humble, but in fact we were being arrogant. Like too many companies, we imposed our own 'intelligence' and 'insight' on the simple, straightforward needs of the customer. Three months later, they fired us, as they should have. We didn't listen."

Clark found out what happens when a business sets everything up for itself, not for the customer. We try to force the customer to do things the way we want them to happen rather than the other way around. Think about how you can adapt to that and strive to find ways to do business with your customers that work for them. Start by asking some good questions, and *listen* to the answers.

I love what Joe Pulizzi, content marketing evangelist, said he does: "I ask my customers, 'What keeps you up at night?' Those answers drive our business. Whenever I get inspired by a customer comment, I pass it on to the staff immediately." Tony Nethercutt, general manager North America at Mojiva, Inc., says he encourages the team members to "both encourage their clients to do what we think should be done as well as ask questions like 'If our offering could do one thing to really help your business, what would it be?'" But Russ Mann, CEO of Covario, knows that just doing what the customer says isn't the best thing, either: "What they say they want and what they actually buy are often very different things, and sometimes it's not a matter of what, but when." Good questions help you find the right answers.

Simply put, there is just no substitute for listening to your customers and then *keep listening*, because as Kent Huffman, chief marketing officer at BearCom Wireless Worldwide, says, "If you do, they'll tell you exactly what they want and need, which in turn will enable you to make the changes necessary to turn those customers into rabid proponents for your company." That's the most important step in turning customers into brand ambassadors—Apple-like fanatics who will walk over burning coals to sing your praises and testify to others with definitive conviction that they should do business with you, too.

Chapter 28

The customer is always in charge. Engage customers on this level in social media and dare to be radically transparent.

I saw another "F***you" on the wall. I tried to rub it off with my hand. . . . It wouldn't come off. It's hopeless, anyway. If you had a million years to do it in, you couldn't rub out even half the "F***you" signs in the world. It's impossible.

—Holden Caulfield, in
The Catcher in the Rye, by J. D. Salinger

My son and I were out riding our horses when my horse, Blaze, stopped at the edge of a shallow creek. My son and his horse had already crossed, but Blaze wouldn't budge. That's how I found out Blaze does not like the water. I'm trying everything to get him to cross when all of a sudden he crouches down really low and he *leaps* across the creek like we've gone over a steeplechase gate. With my 270 pounds on him, that's quite a feat. I'm gripping the reins and holding tight until we land and he slows down. I started screaming at my son, "Did you see that? Did you see that? I stayed on! I stayed on!"

When you're in the saddle, there are times when you need to hold on for dear life, and that's kinda what it feels like in social media every day. If you don't feel this way most of the time, you're doing something wrong. Change your approach and put yourself and your business out there completely, or get out. Sure, you'll miss out on an essential and powerful tool for connecting with your customers, but nothing pisses customers off more than your being out there but being inconsistently responsive.

What else is there to say? Like so many others, I speak and blog frequently about the value of social media, and I devoted a large chunk of *The Mirror Test* to it. (I included that book's four social media Es for customer relations—engage, educate, excite, and evangelize—in this book's Appendix B. You're welcome.) There are no social media secrets anymore. No packaging or advertising, from marketing materials to commercials, fails to include at least a Facebook page. And every event has a social media component, with Twitter, texting, and beyond to engage the customers. It's not just Super Bowl–like events, either: I gave a speech in Toronto and tweeted in advance that I was going to do something special and to pay attention. Before I went on, I posted that when I say "return on ignoring," the first person who screams "itracks!" gets $15,000 in free research from itracks. Fifteen people stood up, and I know I saw a dozen more curse that they missed it.

For all the reasons given, I don't need more than a few lines and the rest of this short chapter to tell you what you need to change in order to grow bigger in social media: get out there if you're not, get out there in full if you are, and when you get there, *be* there and dare to be radically transparent.

Companies that once thought they controlled their brands are realizing that social media is the new norm. It's not about catchy slogans. No more hiding behind 800-number phone trees and website labyrinths—it's about listening and being radically transparent. So what is radical transparency? It means you need to be genuine in your approach. Don't just spew forth information. Social media is about hearts and minds, not ears and eyeballs. It's about being who you are and owning it. If I say "Bite me" in a post, it's because I mean it. You may disagree, or you may not like it. But for me, radical transparency is all about being true to who you are and true to yourself. What works for me is what works for me. It will be different for you—and for everyone else out there as well. That's why it's called "social" media and not "one kind" media. The old rules don't apply in the same way. For as many fans as you have on Facebook or followers on Twitter, there are that many ways it can be done.

And ultimately, we all have a choice in whom we follow or friend. If you don't like what I have to say, you have the choice to not follow me. And we can agree to disagree. At the end of the day, those who follow me know that I'm the big, brash guy from South Dakota who tells it like it is, really wears those cowboy boots, and loves to ride horses. I'm me, and I won't change who I am.

People and companies that are unfailingly genuine, transparent, and real and that do it big and do it well have always succeeded. Now we have a medium that plays to those strengths! So be true to who you are—in social media and in business. Have a personality, and keep giving your customers things to make them come back and check in. Share everything you can. When we developed a social media policy at Kodak, I said, "Share it! Share what we are doing. I don't care if it is an internal document. Who cares? Share it! Because if we don't, someone else will soon enough. We might as well be first at sharing our own policy!" Kodak's social media policy was not a design for the next big thing, a state secret, or insider trading info. It was just a bunch of stuff about blogging, Facebook, Twitter, and what we do. If we shared it, people would talk about it. They'd say, "This is great! Look what they've done. These guys get it!"

So share it! Be creative and have some fun, sure, but engage your attackers, too. Face and respond to them on Yelp and Gripe and other customer complaint sites that spring up, and invite them inside yours. They're not like vampires, and they're coming in anyway, especially when your company is doing all the sucking. A big part of being transparent is being honest. It can't all be about selling, passing along information, and good news. Social media is a great place to say, "We suck!" when something sucks. It's the last place to stay silent or cover it up; it's where you want to own it. Wear your integrity like a heart on your social media sleeve.

Amazingly, big companies are more adept at this than small businesses. Look at what Dell did with Dell Hell: the company had a problem and owned it. It's one thing if your customers use social media to complain. It's another thing if you do it first! And you know what? Your employees and your customers love that! They love that you are human. So what if some people don't like you or your stuff or think you suck? Now they can tell you to your face . . . I mean feed. And you can respond.

The big problems people and companies have with social media have to do first with trying something different and then with radical transparency. They are terrified about giving up control of the brand to the customer. Well, let me know when you decide to enter the twenty-first century. Customers have always been in charge, but now with social media, they expect to be! And if you don't give them control, they can use their own platforms and any number of sites and tools to tell "the world." And there is absolutely nothing you can do about it. We want business the way they want it, and the social media has given us that. And you want that! *So* many companies spend time and money on search engine optimization (SEO), and I think that's very important. So, obviously, companies want customers to find them—now let them find the real you!

And make sure the real you uses social media well. How we use social media is as important as how we use any other medium—print, Web, video, broadcast, podcast—an essential tool in a toolbox that is changing every day. But just because social media makes everyone a tweet away, do not assume you are connected and using social media well. I imagine almost anyone reading this has a website, a Facebook page, Twitter and LinkedIn accounts, and a blog. Can you tell me the difference between the conversations and interactions you have there?

- LinkedIn is like your storefront on Main Street, where people like to browse.

- Blogs are like a public diary on any topic you want posted on bulletin boards all over town.

- Facebook is like a living room where you can have longer and deeper kinds of conversations and interactions, but to do so, you need to sit down and stay for a while.

- Twitter is like your front porch cum cocktail party, where quick and easy conversations happen and people tell people what other people said.

Each of these social media sites has generally accepted practices, and you and your company can say and post anything you want as long as you stay within the scope of those practices and, I'll say it again, are transparent about why you are there. There's nothing wrong with selling something if your followers expected that. But if they follow you for friendship and you send them solicitations? That's bad form. You can do it, but you will not be invited back. And once you are out there, don't forget to listen, too. Radical transparency is *not* a one-way street of engagement. Let your customers educate you, and look for ideas and innovation through them.

Today, I'm online at least an hour every day, looking, posting, and responding. At Kodak, I needed to hire a chief listening officer to manage some of the chaos and comments on our social media sites around the world and to route information from Twitter and blogs to the right people. How do you do it when you're smaller? The same way, just on a smaller, but still dedicated, scale. On the most basic level, radical transparency—like social media as a whole—requires only time and the right attitude to succeed.

Friendsourcing the Rule of Thirds

Does everyone "get" social media? Of course not. Like so many marketing and media tools, it all comes down to my "Rule of Thirds." For everything—marketing programs, initiatives, and beyond:

- A third of the people will get it immediately.

- A third of the people will get it eventually.

- A third of the people will never get it.

In the old marketing models, you never worried too much about the last third; you just told people what you had and what it was about. In the age of social media, you have a responsibility to engage and at least try to educate all of them. Ignoring them no longer means they ignore you. Social media even works to connect people in businesses that are polar opposites. Arnold Kahn, president of PrintLink (which places people in the printing and graphics business), told me, "Social media transformed our business dramatically. We discovered new ways of connecting with people in our industry who would not necessarily reach out to us conventionally."

Several change agents I spoke to bravely admitted they had missed the boat initially on social media, but turned it around quickly. That's the beauty of social media, too. As long as you eventually get it, you can catch up pretty quickly. And you don't need some high-priced consultant to get started. I've heard too many people tell me—as if it were a *good thing*—that they are throwing 30 to 40 percent of their marketing budget into social media—not SEO and other quantifiable tools, but social media. What? First of all, *The Mirror Test* and countless good blogs and books offer techniques to improve your business outreach using social media. Maybe you need to update your hardware and software and other tools you use. But if you can't take the time to do it yourself, why hire someone to change this? You are your own listening officer first, and if you can't or won't commit to social media yourself, why do it at all? Seems to me you'll never get it.

Establish a Focused Executive Program that delivers top-to-top, one-to-one strategic relationships that target your top customers.

The holy grail of sales and marketing is the one-to-one relationship, and this grail is easier to find if you are consistent, always persistent, and follow through with your customers. So get out there and build strong one-to-one relationships, establish your credibility, and deliver great results! If there is a better way to grow satisfied customers, gain their respect, and close sales to generate positive revenue than this holy grail, I am not aware of it. Strive to do this on a continual basis. Let's use every tool we have to keep our products and services relevant to existing and potential customers.

Now that's a rousing speech! Great for your front lines, huh? But if you think this is the point where I say, "Go give it to them!" you are as mistaken as the people who said no one would ever want a horseless carriage, the paper that announced, "Dewey Beats Truman," and the Yankee fans who popped champagne in the ninth inning of game four against the Red Sox in the 2004 American League Championship (that last one is for my writer, Jim).

Look in the mirror, executives, vice presidents, presidents, owners, C-suiters . . . I'm talking to *you*. Customer service is all about the one-to-one relationships, and while no one can or should do it all, it cannot all be left to the front lines once the deals are done.

When I stepped in as chairman of the online research firm itracks.com, the first thing I did was ask for a list of its top 20 customers. I peppered my itracks team with questions about those customers: How much business did they do last year? How much business will they do this year? How do we get close to them and help them (because if I help them grow, I can have more business)? Then I asked to go see them. Sure, itracks was asking these questions and connecting to a certain extent, but like many good companies, not to the extent it should have been. I would change that. "Hi, I'm Jeff Hayzlett, and I'm the new chairman, and I'm coming to see you. How's it going? What can I do for and with you? How can I help you grow your business? What are your biggest problems?"

I needed to do all this work because itracks had not yet implemented my essential top-level tool for growth—a formal change in your way of communicating with top customers and in your attitude when dealing with them: the Focused Executive Program.

A Focused Executive Program comes down to one word: *relationships*. So get off your butt, get out from behind your goshdarned desk, and go visit and talk to customers—every single one of you—so they turn to you and you can help them. This is Jeff-speak for something more diplomatic, suitable for pasting into PowerPoint slides anywhere:

* Establish top-to-top executive relationships with key strategic customers.

- Use these relationships, whenever appropriate, to

  - Influence major business decisions.

  - Avoid/assist in crisis management and/or problem resolution.

  - Identify long-term opportunities for collaboration.

Wait, stop. I see you nodding your head in agreement. (I do . . . you think that camera is *really* off?) I'm glad you agree, because this is logical, commonsense stuff—and that's exactly why you're probably not doing it. Like itracks, you *think* you're doing this. But you probably aren't doing it—at least at the level you must. And if you think you are (even if you are just a company of one), you're *still* probably not doing it. Unless your words and deeds match those of a Focused Executive Program, stop the nodding and change!

And get comfortable. Explaining this one takes a little longer than usual.

The Goal of a Focused Executive Program

The goal of a Focused Executive Program is to establish top-to-top strategic relationships—one-to-one relationships that connect at the top of a business's food chain. You want to be seen as your customer's partner and even a thought leader for your customer's business, something that is not possible when only salespeople and lower-level executives are responsible for all communications.

Why You Need It

Does this sound familiar? Your top salesperson or a key front-line person who is responsible for important, high-level accounts quits. Good companies have nondisclosure and noncompete agreements to cover any potential external problems. But what about your customers? They liked that person. They knew and relied on that person at your company. They had a *relationship* with that person. That means you have a hole. Or what if the same relationship existed, but your employee had (despite your best efforts) declined in her ability and needed to go? Or what if the employee is someone that you love and that you think does an excellent job, but a key customer just doesn't like that person? You have the same hole.

That's when executives usually get or need to make "the call" from or to a freaked-out customer who wants to know what you are going to do to make this right. Now, what if you had already taken the steps to make it right *before* this call happened? What if your top people had already established relationships with your customers, and you actually *wanted* your customers to call those top people and share the pain of this and any other major changes in their business? What if your customers knew this? That's a whole new level of customer satisfaction. That's a deep relationship that avoids the traditional traps of bottom-to-top communication, namely, that the frontline people do all the communicating with your customers once you start doing business with them.

At a company as large as Kodak, but really at any company, many senior people know the big customers by name, but never see them—different divisions often have no connection with one another. With a Focused Executive Program, they will. That's smart. Now people above teams and divisions will know the importance of a particular customer or business and can help solve problems and, better yet, proactively accelerate long-term business opportunities with that customer.

How It Works

In a Focused Executive Program, everyone in the company spans "silos"— not just change agents. Senior *nonsales, non-day-to-day account people* establish relationships with key customers by meeting with them face to face in person (not via video) once or twice a year. This should involve *all* senior people in your company. I mean, why not have your HR chief, finance director, head of Legal, and any other executives in the company outside of Sales travel to see your biggest customers? Sure, those people have internal customers, too, but this reminds all of them that they ultimately work for the external customers. And how hard is it for the head of Accounting to meet with a customer twice a year and keep an open line to that customer year-round? Have you even asked these people to do it? My experience is, they come back energized and full of ideas and great information—excited to have been involved.

DESIGN, APPROACH, AND REPORTING BACK

A Focused Executive Program must connect to the values of your company and should connect to the operational processes laid out earlier in the book. For example, at Cenveo, our Focused Executive Program meant mobilizing our employees around SOAR (Superior operations, One company, Align resources, Replicate success) and deploying total company selling to grow our market share. At Kodak, it meant reminding everyone that a FAST (Focus, Accountability, Simplicity, Trust) mindset means treating everyone as customers—especially our customers—and ensuring that we understand their needs, deliver as agreed and without excuses, embrace innovation, and exceed their expectations continuously.

A Focused Executive Program then follows a pretty standard course (get that PowerPoint slide ready); it works best if one person coordinates it all, including the liaison with Sales:

- Identify and target your top corporate strategic partners.

- Set a schedule for training and contact.

- Develop a standard process for those connections that includes benchmarks.

- Assign senior people to your top customers.

- Implement and integrate the program with a consistent process and questions.

- Make introductions and arrange for face-to-face contact at least twice a year.

- Report back and liaise with Sales.

- Keep the door open year-round.

And when I say assign senior people to your top customers, I mean *all* your senior people, from the CEO down (at Kodak, we had 400 executives, and we made sure each one had at least one account). Don't let anyone skip the training, either; train everyone involved so they all know what to do and what the conditions of satisfaction are. The agenda is the questions I asked earlier when I started at itracks (How's it going? What can I do for and with you? How can I help you grow your business? What are your biggest problems?), but the conversation should be fluid and natural. And make sure your people present what they discussed to the whole team.

That's how you make everyone in a Focused Executive Program accountable to one another and ultimately to the customers. That's teamwork.

Okay, I Get the Benefits, but Nothing's This Easy . . . What Are the Problems and Pitfalls?

You're right. The businesses I worked for and with learned and gained much from the diverse senior people's different perspectives.

They loved doing the program, not just implementing it. And the top customers *loved* it, too; they got the benefits immediately. It made them feel important, as I knew it would—a similar program made me feel important when I was a customer. These programs make doing business like dealing with a friend—someone you trust. (At Kodak, I had four clients assigned to me. I still go hunting with two of them.)

The key to making the program work is focused and ongoing implementation, which is its main pitfall. It's best to start small to work out the kinks and understand the commitments involved, and then expand the scope and scale over time. (At Kodak, for example, we started in the graphics division and worked forward from there.) This also gets a few senior people on board to support the broader implementation and explain what is involved. After all, your senior people need to be available for follow-up and strategic counsel on a regular basis—not just twice a year. And they must report to your salespeople and your leadership team whenever there is contact. This means more work, and the time commitment is always a problem in things like these. Make your people make time for this, but make sure you are as efficient as possible first.

In addition, it is very likely that your salespeople and others on the front line won't like the program at first. They want control of the customer, and they may think you do not trust them. But when you explain that the person doing the connecting is not doing any day-to-day work and is not directly responsible for sales, eventually they get it. The senior people in no way want to be or should be cc'd on any process or regular correspondence. In other words, there's no competition. It's more about opening doors *for* sales to grow bigger.

But even then, with all these efficiencies and permissions in place, don't expect—don't *ever* expect—that everyone will get it. Remember: no program, no matter how popular it is or how much revenue it generates, ever gets everyone aligned in support. It comes down to that rule of thirds: a third of your people will get it right away, a third of your people will eventually get it, and a third of your people will never get it at all—even if they are forced to do it. I remember at Kodak, some people fought us the whole time. Some argued they already did it. (Of *course* they did!)

But I have found that with a Focused Executive Program, more people than usual eventually get it, especially after meeting with a customer. Then, we couldn't stop them.

AND IN THE END . . .

If you want to be a customer-driven company and you deal with businesses as customers, then a Focused Executive Program is something you ought to do. It can make any size business feel like a small company. But as I said, even small businesses can miss the point of the program. They can get distracted as much as a big business and leave their frontline people in charge of all the day-to-day business. A Focused Executive Program gives you a way to stay, well, focused at the top. It's a business-to-business squeeze for your customers. It says to them, "I'm going to go overboard for you. It's all about you. Gimme a hug." I don't know a business in the world—big or small—that gets closer to its customers like this and doesn't reap huge benefits.

Here's a real-money analogy to leave you with: casino owners and the senior people who work for them know all their biggest customers—their "whales"—personally. They know the second the whales walk in the door and when they hit the floor, and at that moment, the owner or the most senior person available is there welcoming them, shaking hands, making sure their needs are met, and doing anything he can to make their experience more enjoyable. Casinos know the money isn't just in the bets; it's in the one-to-one relationships.

Friendsourcing Focus

R emember how I said that a FAST operational process treats everyone like a customer? Keith Larson, president of structurIT Worldwide, told me a story from his previous company about the perils of not focusing on all your customers, in the broadest definition of that term: "We were trying to make a finance-driven company change into a sales-driven company. There was so much attention on the customers and the internal politics that all of the other stakeholders were not being taken care of. Unexpectedly, one of the major shareholders sold their shares to a new investor. This started a fire that led to a hostile takeover of the company. We had not made sure all of the stakeholders were on board and focused too much on internal activities."

Several friends also recalled how we mobilized our team at Cenveo in a rapidly changing environment by transforming our business from a top-down organization to one that was organized from the bottom up, or, as we liked to say, "right side up." A right-side-up company flips its traditional organizational model to serve the needs of the customer first, followed by the frontline employees, managers and supervisors, and finally the senior people:

Top-Down Hierarchy of Importance	Right-Side-Up Hierarchy of Importance
Senior executives/C-suite	Customers
Managers and supervisors	Frontline employees
Frontline employees	Managers and supervisors
Customers	Senior executives/C-suite

An organizational structure like this directly complements a Focused Executive Program and all your evolving customer service work by reinforcing one-to-one relationships with your customers at the top *and* the front lines of your organization. In the right-side-up reorganization, managers communicate, set direction, coach, and remove barriers by training the frontline employees. They seek to understand what these people do by asking questions similar to the ones your senior people ask your top customers in the Focused Executive Program: How can I help you do your job better? How can I empower you to make decisions and take actions? How can I help you commit to achieving winning results? This gives the frontline employees the knowledge, experience, and capability and reinforces their commitment to achieving those winning results (that is, solving problems and increasing sales and profits).

At Cenveo, we created a focus document to support this right-side-up approach: a two-page document outlining the mission, values, strategy, goals, and measurements for the entire company. It communicated in clear, lucid terms what the objective was: to grow market share while achieving and sustaining a return on capital employed, or ROCE, in excess of 20 percent. It spelled out the goals, the rules of the game, and a measurement system or scorecard for evaluation. It focused on, well, the focus of the plan, which in Cenveo's case was a transformation from a collection of independent companies into "one great company." And like the Focused Executive Program, it tied all of this back into our values as defined by SOAR.

The point of a focus document is not to change your measurement systems (hopefully, you've read *The Mirror Test* and spelled out how success will be calculated and measured). The point is to support a change to right side up in everything you do and to put all the measurements and detail into supporting one mission: helping your customers. The result? An organization that focuses on the customer and listens from bottom to top.

Chapter 30

Stampedes lead to fast results, but they're expensive and exhausting. Create scalable plans that unfold as you grow.

Two virile bulls, one young and one old, are sitting on a hill looking down at a pasture full of cows. The young bull looks at the old one and says, "Old man, I say we run down this hill and make love to all those cows." The old one shakes his head. "Nope, I say we *mosey* on down and make love to all of them one by one."

Okay, maybe the cowgirls won't like that analogy, but bulls have played an important part in our change story before, and the analogy here is just as important. Stampeding down a hill the way the young bull wants to often leads to results and market share fast, but at what expense? There's no way you can sustain it and satisfy all your customers at once. The older bull knows that stampeding compromises the quality of his performance, the availability of his resources, and his ability to keep on delivering on the promise to his customers—big sacrifices in the name of speed and making a huge initial impact. For the most part, that just doesn't work, either in life or in business.

"Young bull" marketing plans waste your and your business's energy and money. They stampede into awareness on the backs of huge, expensive, one-off plans that require massive resources (not just money, but people and time) to execute again and again and again. It's much easier on your bottom line to follow the old bull's way and launch aggressively, but with a more targeted focus on your customers that builds momentum and gains mind share over time. It's also easier to keep your people, your customers, and yourself involved, motivated, and enthusiastic on a ride that unfolds over time. One single, intense rush is fun while it lasts, but then it's gone. What's next? You're out of money, you're dog-tired, and you still have a long way to go to make sure all your customers are aware of you and that you can deliver on your brand promise and value proposition.

The moral of the story is: don't be "bullied." Change the model by creating scalable plans that unfold as you grow.

I called scale the new black in *The Mirror Test*, and I encourage you to go back, reread that chapter, and rethink all your plans in terms of scale. I won't repeat what I said in that chapter here except to give you a new example of the power of scale and to remind you that the foundation of scale is all about zeros. Just add or take away zeros and any small or big business plan can be drawn to scale. The old model requires you to bull-y your way into the market or use your purchasing power to buy space and people. Big Ink did that by deciding to give away its printers for free; Facebook does this by buying employees for millions, often by purchasing those employees' start-ups and shutting them down. Is this sustainable? Probably not. Does that mean you can't compete? Absolutely not. You just need your team members to work together and innovate, control, and lead by creating marketing programs that offer a more complete and scalable experience.

At Kodak, the program we created was the Kodak Challenge (http://www.KodakChallenge.com), a yearlong virtual golf tournament created around the sponsorship of 24 of the most difficult individual holes at 24 PGA Tour tournaments. These holes make up the Kodak Challenge, and the best 18-hole player wins $1 million.

But to have the time and budget to launch the Kodak Challenge, we needed to change the model at Kodak: to end our affiliation with NASCAR, and to kill our most sacred of cows—Kodak's sponsorship of the Olympics. It was George Eastman himself who made the decision in 1896 to be the first company ever to sponsor the Olympic Games, and we took it away in 2007.

I remember talking to my CEO (I was the chief business development officer at the time) and telling him we needed to step away from the Olympics. I said that without film, we could never sell enough cameras to cover the $50 million that it cost to sponsor each Olympics. Sure, in the age of cameras that needed more and more film to snap their Kodak Moments, the investment had paid dividends, with lots of product being sold. But Kodak was now mostly a business-to-business company, and sponsoring any predominantly business-to-consumer event was just not worth it for us. No one in the track and field audience was going to buy a commercial printer; no one at gymnastics was likely to be thinking about our amazing printing plates. (The Olympics platform, just like a Super Bowl ad, can still offer a value proposition for business-to-consumer businesses like McDonald's, Coca-Cola, or Anheuser-Busch).

My CEO called the decision momentous, and I agreed, which is why we worked to end our relationship well and not offend anyone. Ending the NASCAR relationship was harder for me. I am a big fan of NASCAR. Kodak sponsored a Penske car, and I can't think of any business executive I respect more than Robert Penske. The NASCAR sponsorship was expensive, but, unlike the Olympics, it was good at increasing business on the business-to-business level (a lot of Kodak's graphic arts customers were affiliated with and enjoyed NASCAR). It was a very big motivator to take people to our hospitality events, which we called "closing events" because we took only customers that were about to close a certain level of business. NASCAR was all about business development and growing the business bigger.

That's why the team that pitched the idea of the Kodak Challenge—led by Steven Powell and Terry Clas—was nervous about presenting the idea to me. They thought I would be angry about giving up NASCAR and losing such a positive experience and millions in business development. So what did I say?

"We're gonna miss NASCAR." In fact, I told them they had done a great job. I wished I'd thought of it. But I sure as hell stole it as soon as they came up with it. (I tell them that to their faces to this day.)

Did it matter that I loved NASCAR and hated playing golf? Did it matter that the businesses, like film, that most benefited from NASCAR would lose a major revenue-generating source? No. Remember: *no* process or program can seduce a change agent—that's how people become part of the problem: they get wedded to the way things are. I knew immediately how valuable the Kodak Challenge could be for our brand. It shifted the way our customers were going to perceive us, and it made us more visible to our biggest business-to-business clients. Our business-to-business customers were members at the places where these tournaments were played, which meant Kodak was effectively narrowcasting its message.

The Kodak Challenge is a prime example of creating something eminently scalable, where innovation and control really pay off more than dropping a wad of cash on the table. Kodak gained mind share by generating countless mentions of its name year-round (every time a golfer in one of the 24 tournaments plays one of our holes, the announcer mentions that it's part of the Kodak Challenge). Fans track the quest for the million-dollar prize on

KodakChallenge.com. And since we chose many back-nine holes, we were assured coverage at many televised tournaments. Plus, the idea is easy to add on to. Kodak can expand to majors or add more local tournaments, work with pros around the country, and create fantasy leagues.

Customers get involved, too. Greenside tents stocked with cameras let people take photos of the play and post their "Kodak Moment" pictures on KodakChallenge.com, as well as on Facebook and other social networking sites. Fans can also post pictures of the various tournaments or of themselves playing at one of the selected holes. They blog their opinions of the various players or the holes and root for their favorites. They're actually participating in the Kodak Challenge, rather than just staring at a sign.

How much did all this cost? The entire Kodak Challenge, despite the logistics and extra manpower needed to run it, costs less than the price of sponsoring a single PGA Tour tournament and less than 20 percent of the Olympics. For every dollar Kodak puts in, it gets 10 times the visibility and exposure. (While I was at Kodak, only our sponsorship of an episode of *Celebrity Apprentice* and the Oscars at the Kodak Theater got more impressions, and they were once-a-year events.) Steven and Terry showed us the way by delivering dollar-for-dollar the best-run sponsorship in major league sports and the best expenditure of sports sponsorship in the world. It became our new "old bull" model.

Now, Kodak had some zeros to invest in this for sure, and your business might not. But keep this in mind: growth is not measured by the number of zeros you start with, but by how effectively you use the zeros you have to take control of the physical and virtual space you can claim through an event or program. Have fewer zeros? Look for ways to create "events within events" to generate a buzz that is much greater than what you would get by simply sponsoring the whole thing. Sponsor the ninth hole of the most popular golf course in town for a month and track the best scores or the longest drives for a prize. It does not have to be golf—it can be anything that allows your brand to connect with your customers and then gives those customers a chance to interact and spread the word for you. When it succeeds, you repeat it and, when you can, scale it up.

Chapter 31

Never compromise on creativity when you know it is the right thing to do for your brand and your customers.

The *Boston Globe* loved everything about Kodak's new pocket video camera, the Zi8. Well, almost everything. It loved everything *except* the name. Which sucked. In fact, the writer hated it so much he had made it the opening of his amazing review: "When Kodak needed a name for its new pocket video camera, its marketing geniuses came up with something dreadful: the Zi8. Happily, the name's the only thing about it that's lame."

And what marketing genius had come up with the name? Well, I wasn't the one who started naming our products the A series, the B series, and so on (*thank God* we had gotten to Z), but I had to step forward as the "marketing genius" and take this reviewer's bullet. I was the company CMO. I had to take responsibility. No excuses.

And this marketing genius wanted to know one thing: what were we going to do about it?

I printed out the article and ran downstairs to find the team, grabbing everyone I could see. (At these moments, my team would invoke the Hayzlett Proximity Rule: "Don't make eye contact, or he will assign something to you.") We gathered in the conference room.

"Look at this article," I said, shaking the paper. "Look at this article! I told you, we have got the greatest product in the world—a great product. Everyone will want one of these for Christmas. And then we go and name it the Zi8. It sucks." I stopped to read them the opening of the article again.

"So what are we going to do?"

Someone immediately said we should run a contest for our customers to name the next one as a tie-in with next year's Consumer Electronics Show (CES). Next, someone said we should make the contest a true crowdsourcing—announce it and take submissions through our blog and Twitter. Now we're rolling. We decide that the person who submits the winning name will be dubbed the mother or father of the product. We'll put his or her picture on the box (or in it, if he or she has a face for radio). We'll take this person to CES press conferences, and I'll put my arms around him or her. Contest, crowdsourcing, social media, CES . . . all great.

"Let's do it," I said. "Get everybody together now and figure out how we can do it. How many days do we have before we have to go through the product clearance on the names?"

"Seven days," came the answer.

Not much. "Okay, let's go. Fast."

That's when someone said, "But Jeff, we don't have Legal's permission and approval. We need to get that. We have someone who's in charge of contests."

Until that moment, I am not sure I understood in full the meaning of the expression "my jaw hit the floor." I turned to the person next to me and said, "What the hell do you mean we have someone who's in charge of contests?" I looked around the room. "We have a person at our company who's just in charge of contests? Are you kidding me? I want that friggin' job."

We submitted our request to Legal. And then waited. And waited. Hey people, time is money! We had only seven days to solicit the names. Time was slipping away. We said we were going to run a cool contest that could get us tons of customer response and publicity. And all Legal kept saying was that we couldn't run it because we didn't have the time to get permission, and if we didn't get permission, we'd get a fine for not getting permission.

This is the time in stories like these when leaders face an important choice: fold reasonably because someone else says it's the right thing to do, or act on what you believe because you *know* it's the right thing to do. Unfortunately, in these situations, most people think they must take the former route—the path of least resistance, the rational way—even when they know it will kill their best ideas and creative instincts.

Change agents must learn to resist this vile temptress and refuse to compromise on creativity when they believe it's the right thing to do. We did this with the Kodak Challenge and the PGA Tour, refusing to be tied to older sponsorship models like NASCAR and the Olympics. This was another kind of issue: challenging a procedural hurdle. That's not to say that you shouldn't start by trying to follow procedure most of the time. We did. We had only a week to act, but, as much as I hate process for process's sake, we had followed procedure and asked for permission first. That's a good litmus test for the value of your idea, no matter how big or small it may be: it cannot compromise your principles of who or what you are, even if it violates the procedures you have in place. Nothing was hidden from Kodak. If we had had the time, we would not have been rejected for being out of line with our brand principles or values.

But in this case, the idea of folding was impossible. We knew we had a huge opportunity and a brand- and customer-focused idea. We just had no time to do it the "right way." I'd asked for permission; now I might have to beg for forgiveness to see things through.

That's how I ended up thinking, "Well, how much could the fine *be*? How much? $50,000? Could I live with $50,000?" At Kodak, I could. "Go," I phoned the team. "Hit the tweet."

I can't say I had time to think about any consequences after that. In the four days we had left, we got thousands upon thousands of names submitted—names from customers who told us what they wanted to call the product. This is what social media allows you to do and why you work so hard to engage those customers on an ongoing basis—so they are there to help and to be there for your brand. Our customers engaged us. Heck, they sent out 27,000 tweets of their own—they evangelized! In just four days, we had more people visit and put a name on our website than we had had people visit us in the entire *history* of our website.

And I made sure the writer at the *Boston Globe* saw our contest too and knew we agreed with him. He quickly posted a second story with the headline, "Is There a Better Name than the Zi8? Then Go Tell Kodak."

Next week, the form came down from Legal. The fine was $300.

Adapt or die! Change is not an end in itself, but a chance to expand on success and to understand the "boomerang effect" of change.

A friend of mine went to his doctor to get something removed from his face near his eye. The doctor put him in a chair, tilted him back, and focused the light. That's when my friend saw the pair of medical scissors in his doctor's hands coming toward him.

"Hey! Hey! Wait, doc, just the scissors? That's gonna hurt, isn't it?"

"Well, yeah, a little bit."

"Well, don't you think you want to give me a shot or something around there to dull the pain? That would be good, right?"

"Well, sure," his doctor said. "I can do that for you if you'd like."

The doctor pulled a needle out of the drawer for the anesthetic.

"Hey! Hey! Wait, doc! What's that needle gonna feel like?"

"About the same as the scissors."

Now consider what happened a number of years ago when the company I worked with noticed a demand for cheaper commercial color printing. We responded with an innovation: an inkjet system that produced cheaper color documents, but at a lower quality than "offset class" (the class most commercial printers and the people they served used for their brochures and glossy materials). Our color was noticeably fuzzier, and we were unsure of how our customers would react. Would they see the value? Would it satisfy the need? Would the difference cost us?

We were getting so caught up in questions about what might happen we were forgetting to make it happen. We went out to our top customers and showed them what we had, and we found that it was plenty good enough for the kind of printing it was designed to do: statements, invoices, bills, receipts . . . items that needed color, but did not need expensive, crystal-clear quality. Everyone in the company celebrated, but I still knew we had a problem: what to name it. If you change or create a business model, you need to define what it is clearly in order to sell it. So, what would we call our new class of inkjet quality?

That's when I came up with the term *business color* and presented it to the team.

A naysayer stepped in immediately: "Business color? Why call it business color?"

"Because you can't sell 's****y color,'" I replied.

Finally, let me tell you about a time I went hunting with some friends in South Dakota. We had taken out the horses and some dogs and were riding across the scrub prairie looking for coveys of sharp-tailed grouse. The dogs look for the coveys and flush them out, and then you get off the horses behind the dogs and shoot.

After a few ups and downs from the saddle, one of my friends from back east said, "Hey, Jeff, can I shoot off the back of this horse?"

"Sure, you can shoot off that horse."

When the dogs flushed out the next covey, my friend stayed on his horse, put the gun to his shoulder, and fired.

And the horse proceeded to buck him right off. He landed with a loud thud on one side of the horse, and his gun landed on the other. Then his horse took off running.

Lying on his back, he looked up at me and said, "Jeff, I thought you said I could shoot off the back of this horse."

"I said you *could.* I didn't say you'd stay on."

What's the moral of these stories? Don't get so caught up in what is going on that you forget to ask the right questions. The right questions are not questions you know the answers to, questions that get you caught up in so much debate (healthy or not) that you fail to act, or questions that are designed to give you the answers you want rather than the answers you need:

- My friend at the doctor got so caught up in fear about the process that he questioned details that in the end didn't make a lick of difference and that distracted both him and the doctor from the goal. *Stop it!* Get it done.

- My friends at the inkjet company got so caught up in questions about whether our process was exactly right that they let the perfect get in the way of the good. No wait, I mean . . . hmm . . . there must be a better way to say that . . . that's such a tired expression . . . maybe . . . *stop it!* It's good enough, and it's not wrong.

- My friend in the saddle didn't ask if he *should* shoot off the horse or if *I would* shoot off the horse. He asked if he could—a question that looked for the answer he wanted and, as a result, got him thrown from the saddle. *Stop it!* Ask whether you *should* do something, not whether you *could*, and learn to ask one question a bunch of different ways before your company gets thrown from the saddle.

And once you learn to do this, you've probably seen some success as a change agent. So there's really only one thing left to say: "Congratulations! Let's do it again." Because here's the truth: details are about the process and the present and can't concern you now. "Good enough" doesn't mean "don't change a thing." And the one question change agents must make sure their companies ask first—the question from which all future questions and changes stem—is, "Why not?" After all, successful organizations know they need to be fluid so they can better respond to changing markets and customer needs—they must adapt or die.

I covered "adapt or die" in *The Mirror Test* and showed how to ask seven specific "adapt-or-die" questions to uncover what you don't know. (See Appendix C for the list. Again, you're welcome.) But in retrospect, I should have started with the mother of all those questions: why not?

In one of the first chapters in this book, I explained that the wrong question to ask at the turn of the twentieth century was, "Who would want a horseless carriage?" The right one? "Why wouldn't everyone want one?" In other words, why not? If I were speaking at the buggy whip convention in 1904, that's exactly what I'd say to the buggy whip folks. I even wrote part of my keynote speech:

> Why not adapt? Pay attention, people! Henry Ford is coming. Be prepared to be the best. Because only one or two of you are going to survive by making buggy whips. And those two are going to specialize. Very soon you are not going to be able to mass-produce whips. You won't be able to sell 100,000 of them a year anymore. Maybe for the next 50 years, there'll still be a business for buggy whips, just not as many. So, you're gonna adapt. You're gonna make them handmade. They've gotta have style so the people who need them will covet your models. The rest of you? You're going

to trade on your good name and realize that what you are is not what you make but what you do. And you do transportation. And while you can't invent the car, drivers already trust you to be part of their driving experience. Change what you make and sell steering wheels and brake pedals to Henry Ford.

I figure this is when the boos would start getting louder, so I'd beat a hasty retreat before the audience got really angry—those people have whips! But I meant every word. I believe those buggy whip people could have survived! Sure, their products wouldn't be going anywhere for long, certainly not on the scale the companies were used to. That does *not* mean they couldn't do it better or adapt in related areas to support the change that was already happening. Remember what I said at the beginning of this part of the book: only some of those in the first wave of '49ers made money striking gold. The rest made money selling maps and tools, girls and grub.

But what if a company has the ability to strike gold? If its leaders don't ask why not, they'll never ask important questions like, "How can we prepare for what's to come, not just focus on what we've achieved so far?" They become Kodak and ignore the digital camera that it invented in 1975 to focus on film. They become GE around the same time, twisting and turning tubes into a tight coil and creating the first compact fluorescent bulb—and then, finding it too expensive to mass-produce, deciding not to license its design.

In the end, change is not an end in itself, but a chance to expand on success. Change offers a chance for businesses to see their markets and their customers in new ways—a chance to consider new strategies, investigate and invest in new technologies, invent new ways of doing business, test things, and more. It's about opportunity—that's what's most appealing about adapt or die. Adapt is always better than die, and businesses are not about dying. Products might be. You can let a product die. Businesses should be more than a product and should never be too beholden to any single product. Anything can become obsolete. Look at movies, books, and mobile communications, changing every day in the way their products are delivered and consumed. If people in these businesses ask why not before obsolescence strikes and can see past their current success to explore innovation and change, they can reclaim that venturesome spirit and either strike gold or sell the tools.

Change means stretching your brand without breaking its promises—widening it and personalizing it while keeping its DNA intact. Stretching your brand is all about standing behind principles when they are inconvenient and fighting to move ahead so the company changes for the better and keeps growing. If you are staying true to the core of who you are, then you can make it, and that doesn't always mean choosing the sexiest path with the most potential customers. If faced with two choices—going down the path with more customers but away from its core values, and going down the path with fewer customers, but staying true to those values—a company should always choose the latter and explore the former by asking why not. Choosing the former is choosing change for change's sake.

And if all this has started to sound very familiar—if it sounds as if I am asking the same questions I asked at the beginning of this book—that's because I am. I'm asking them every single day in every business I work for. Why are we doing this? What are the reasons? What drives us? Adapt or die is as much about progress as it is about going back to the beginning! If you marched around the world, you'd still end up where you began. Every time companies adapt, they go through the change process from the beginning, and this requires them to reset, look to the future, and satisfy present demands at the same time. It's an amazing feat of cognitive dissonance—a state that occurs when your existing beliefs are challenged, requiring you to hold conflicting ideas in your head simultaneously.

Or, as I like to say: change is a boomerang. If you throw a boomerang hard enough and in the right way at the right angle, it will go as far as you can get it before it comes hurtling back to you. Adapt or die is the ultimate point in this boomerang effect—a chance to think about what's next for your company before your changes come hurtling back to where they started.

And then you do it again, asking all the right questions and applying what your company has learned by thinking big and growing bigger. Are there ideas being generated in-house or within your customers' or stakeholders' purview that would help you achieve even greater success? Of course there are, and you have a right-side-up organization to tap those ideas! Are these the employees you want to take with you as you adapt? Go back to the beginning. Use every opportunity to test your people so you can adapt.

And if the answers to all these questions point to die? In the age of planned obsolescence and temporary companies that are Googled—I mean gobbled—up by bigger fish, you will at least be asking the right questions so you know what you can deal with, how and when to stop kidding yourself about what you can do, and fold so you can go out on top!

Friendsourcing Adapt or Die

"Innovation is doing something better that people will pay for. The funny thing is that your existing competition does not stay still, and new competition comes from nowhere—so you have to change." I love that quote from my friend Gary Shapiro, president and CEO of the Consumer Electronics Association and author of an unabashedly conservative but intriguing book, *The*

Comeback: How Innovation will Restore the American Dream. Gary knows a lot about adapting—his industry is in a constant state of change, and his association's trade show, the Consumer Electronics Show (known as CES), has needed to adapt many times in order to thrive. The annual CES in Las Vegas remains a huge success, while its rivals like Comdex have declined or disappeared.

But while I agree the competition in business never stays still, I don't agree that it comes from nowhere. In fact, it comes from everywhere (internationally and domestically), starting with your customers and long before they click to buy. You can innovate and challenge existing models all you want, but if your customers aren't with you to begin with, they will never follow your innovation. And then, if they don't understand your changes even after you've educated them, you will fail. And *then*, if they don't demand what you supply—let alone buy it—your company will die. Today, it's all about the customer.

Smart change agents have always gotten this, particularly those who work in media like my friend Richard Lobel, executive vice president of CBS Radio Altitude Group and CBS RIOT. Radio has faced Kodak film–like challenges from myriad forms of broadcast and streaming media for decades, but, as Richard notes, customers (not the broadcast media) are in control: "Advertisers would say to us that radio is an 'old-fashioned' medium. We didn't accept that. We became an early adopter of streaming and digital technology and rapidly created innovative approaches of distributing our content across a multitude of platforms. Consumers are in control more than ever regarding how, where, and when they want their content. And, we had to satisfy their never-ending thirst for consumer content on their terms."

The key, then, is understanding what these terms are as you adapt and finding a balance between providing the services your customers demand now and anticipating what they will need in the future. Marketers must be extra aware of this, lest they become irrelevant buggy whip dealers. For example, Jeff Cleary is the owner and managing director of Catalyst, which was a traditional direct marketing agency back in the early 1990s. Jeff saw the digital revolution coming and realized his business was "ill-equipped to provide value to our clients going forward unless we reinvented ourselves." But did Jeff and his company abandon print and other existing "old-school" technologies? No. They created an "integrated online and offline marketing model that could effectively target consumers wherever they engaged with brands."

Catalyst, like Kodak, got the talent and services it needed to adapt through hiring and acquisition, and sometimes that is the best choice if you are to grow. Using your resources now to invest for the future is smart, and it's even smarter if it also helps you get out of your own way. My friend Thaddeus B. Kubis, president of NAK Integrated Marketing Inc., wished he had done this when he was facing an economic downturn: "I was overly confident that I could control the dynamics of any economic downturn with my never-before-failed approach and very successful career. I should have looked for outside help to prepare or adapt to the problem."

Of course, not all businesses can or need to hire and acquire in order to adapt and grow; they just need to see the changes coming before it's too late to recover. And I am not just talking about businesses in electronics, software, scientific research, and other areas that must adapt every day. I'm talking about businesses that serve those businesses and satisfy basic everyday customer needs. Mike Steinberg, president and CEO of Relyco: Business Printing & Payment Solutions, has a lucrative business in laser check stock and in-house check printing. However, it's no secret that the need for paper checks is dwindling.

To adapt, Mike built on the DNA of his business (his trusted expertise in payment processing and solutions) to deliver new promises and solutions to his clients. After all, people still need to get paid, and Relyco knew how to do it! As Mike reports, Relyco continues to provide top-quality paper printing products, but it has introduced "alternative [electronic payment and processing] solutions to address this changing market to stay ahead."

Or consider what my friend Steven J. Greenbaum, CEO of PostNet, told me about how he reacted slowly to changes in how franchise buyers purchase businesses and the resulting consequences as his business entered the recent recession: "Many organizations like ours continued to invest in dead or dying prospecting strategies because there were no better ways known, shared, or understood. While innovation is occurring now through a focus on organic prospecting, SEO [search engine optimization], and the development of other measurable nontraditional methods, the organizations' overall sales and momentum were impacted. The great news is that sales are growing again, and we will emerge a better, faster, and smarter company than we were before."

Steven adapted by using new technology and better metrics to create a "more focused, efficient organization, a better business model." In enacting these changes, however, he also realized another essential point that change agents must not miss when the time comes to adapt and start the whole change process over again: the impact these innovations have on your people, whether you fail or succeed. As Steven said to me, "The most important thing to do is assure the troops with extreme clarity in adjusting to current conditions with a vision for the future."

Paul Caine, executive vice president and chief revenue officer of Time Inc., acknowledged the same point about adapting to neutralize the competition: "After many years of limited competition, a significant competitor emerged and started to derail the current business environment and model. The situation created dissension and confusion. We were able to align the team once again by creating shorter-term goals, focusing the language into sound bites so that the entire operation could repeat it with ease, and aligning the strategy across the organization."

In other words, process makes perfect for your people! Or at least good enough so they and you can succeed. Remember: in a right-side-up organization, your people are your customers, too. They need to be with you not only as you change, but also as you change again and again and again.

Chapter 33

Don't get mad.
Don't get even. Just get
ahead and never give up!
Outlast the bastards who
will try to destroy what
you do. Be relentless.

When I started as a lobbyist in South Dakota, the "Big Two" lobbyists didn't like me, because I was winning a lot of business—from them. It wasn't just the money; I was changing the way these two lobbyists did business by cutting them out. Before I came along, they had run the machine: people came to them with the causes they wanted lobbied, and the Big Two doled out the business to the other lobbyists, taking their cut first. As a result, everyone was beholden to them—except me. Honestly, I didn't know any better. I was new at this game, and I didn't have time to wait for business to come to me. So, I just went out and found it, recruiting customers by visiting them, presenting my services, and listening to what they needed.

After my first lobbying successes during the main legislative period, I won a lot more business, and the Big Two had had enough. They didn't like the money I was making, they didn't like the success I was having, and they especially didn't like it when people started showing up and asking them, "Are you Jeff Hayzlett?" Oh, that really pissed them off. That's when they decided to get even with me with a prank. Before the biggest and most important cocktail party of the season, they made buttons that said, "I'm not Jeff Hayzlett," brought them to the event, and had everyone put them on. They must have thought that seeing all those buttons around the room would anger me. But when I showed up and saw the buttons, I realized what was happening.

I found a Magic Marker, walked right up to the Big Two, very calmly took a button, crossed out the *not*, and put the button on.

"I *am* Jeff Hayzlett," I said and walked away.

I walked around that party that evening wearing my button with pride. I never engaged the instigators, reacted to all the other buttons, or asked anyone to take a button off. I never acted the way they wanted me to. As I said earlier, it doesn't make sense to get caught up in attacking the people who are attacking you; it's better to ignore them and pretend that they're not there. If I had played their game, they could have controlled the rules. I played my own game and did not back down.

This experience has served me well throughout my career as a change agent. I have learned to resist the siren calls of naysayers, opportunists, and obstructionists who try to shipwreck my causes. The hundreds and hundreds of times I had some version of this conversation has made me strong:

"This is how we're supposed to do it," *they* would say.

"I don't care," I would reply.

"But . . ."

"I don't. Does the way we're '*supposed* to do it' seem right to you?"

"No."

"Well, then, if it's not right, why are we doing it that way?"

My attitude wasn't about disobeying the rules; it was about changing the rules for the better—sometimes the very rules I had put in place years before when I first started changing things! I'm not above it all. I never let the way things are done be good enough for anyone, including me. That's why I like laws with sunset provisions. That's why I like to serve on bylaws committees for the boards of the organizations I work with. I like it when things come up for review. I like challenging myself to do it better all the time.

As we put this book together, I told Jim I was more caught up on my work than I had been at any other point in my life. I said that made me happy but itchy . . . for change. Success is always sweet. Few things are more satisfying. But just like the businesses we work for, change agents must always be thinking, "What's next?"

Want to hear what the answer in change agent hell sounds like to me? "Relax, put your feet up, and have a Diet Mountain Dew—you deserve it! Here's a comfy chair and a Five Guys cheeseburger. Your wife will never know! And look, *Patton* is on this huge flat screen. Let's plan a vacation now for the two of you—a nice long one! You can bring your horses . . ."

Sounds like heaven, right? Nope, that's no angel on my shoulder. In movies, TV shows, cartoons, and commercials, it might be the angel saying things like this. But in business, these words represent temptation, and this devil is a disciple of the Lotus Eaters from Greek mythology, who plied visitors to their island with yummy lotus fruit, lulled them to sleep, and trapped them there forever without a care in the world. (Sneaky bastards always disguise my lotus fruit as a cheeseburger.)

There's nothing wrong with treating yourself well and rewarding yourself for a job well done, but change agents know the feeling will, should, and must be fleeting. Would we *like* to have things move along nicely and grow as long as possible? Sure!

There's nothing wrong with settling in a little bit, but not so much that you get lost in what's working and miss what's *not* working—and what's possible! Change agents can't get too comfortable in their success. We must always be looking around, asking questions, and considering options and opportunities, both when things are going really poorly *and* when they're going really well. If we don't, we risk becoming part of the problem by thinking this is the way we should do it from now on.

"Away, devil," commands *my* change angel. "Lead Jeff not into indifference to change!"

"Jeff, Jeff," the angel cries, "it can be better. It can *always* be better. Wake up!"

Change agents must relentlessly and constantly try to make things better to satisfy the mutual conditions of satisfaction for our companies and ourselves. Thus, we are always thinking about change. It is our burden to bear. Don't fight it! I'm constantly doing that, no matter where I am. If I can't apply any more changes in my business's marketing, I look to change Operations or Finance. A lot of times I find myself trying to solve customer service issues for companies I do business with. All change agents do. I said this at the beginning of this book: it's part of our DNA. Wherever I am—a restaurant, the airport, a hotel—I wonder how I might do things differently and make it better. My brain is always wondering, "What if . . . ?" and "Why not?"

For example, I go home to South Dakota twice a year to see a battery of medical professionals to satisfy my wife's curiosity about my death—I mean health. Over a couple of days, I get examined, tested, probed, and prodded by a bunch of doctors and health-care providers, all of them part of the same hospital system. And each office makes me fill out the same forms every time I go—until recently, when I refused to fill them out more than once.

"I know I just filled out the same forms down the hall. I know I did it six months ago, too. I know it's in the system, too, and that all of the offices are connected to the system. So I won't do it. Are you even checking the information I give you on that form? Just ask me the questions and I'll give you the answers."

"That's not how it works."

"Well, is your way working? If it were, you wouldn't ask me to fill out this form. You've got the same information from a bunch of different offices over the last couple of days and also from six months ago sitting on your computer."

"Well, sir, that information might've changed."

"Okay, ask me what, if anything, has changed."

"That's not how it works."

I know they hate me, but I can't help myself. There had to be a better way. So I did what any change agent does: I thought about how they could improve the process and suggested some new ideas.

And then they suggested I go and do something to myself that I am not sure is even possible and is certainly not repeatable in polite company.

I don't mind these moments because they are the consequences of being me. I don't take myself too seriously. I can't! People like me try to make these changes happen, knowing all along that any number of people will stand in the way. No matter how secure I feel, I know someone is taking aim at me. If I took myself too seriously, I'd go crazy with rage.

I also know I will never have ultimate control over the changes I make . . . *never*. Change may be a permanent condition, but change agent is not a permanent position. No matter how much I succeed, there is always room to grow. No matter how big I think I might be, someone is always bigger. I thought being CMO of Kodak was a *big* thing until I realized that GE had to grow about one Kodak a year just to be ahead of the previous year! Sometimes this means move up; sometimes this means move on. (On average, CMOs last fewer than two years at a company.) But there is always more to do somewhere—to think big, grow bigger, and satisfy those mutual conditions of satisfaction.

As Margaret Mead famously said, "Never doubt that a small group of thoughtful, committed [people] can change the world. Indeed, it is the only thing that ever has." Perfect parting words for any change agent. What are you waiting for? Let's go and do it . . . again.

Courage is being scared to death, but saddling up anyway. The song of the change agent is the song of the Dog Soldier. Are you ready? Grow!

Where I come from, the greatest warriors of all time were the Dog Soldiers. They were the Michael Jordans of their time. Well, more like Michael Jordan mixed with some Chuck Norris and a healthy dose of gladiator blood.

Many people tried to become Dog Soldiers, but only a handful had the necessary toughness, bravery, skills, and heart. They were a Native American tribe's best offense and last line of defense, in battle and in life. They were charged with serving and protecting the villages by guarding the camps and providing shelter to the needy, food to the hungry, and clothing to those in need. They led tribes and villages from one hunting ground to the next and protected the rear of the tribe from surprise attacks.

The Dog Soldiers carried special arrows—arrows that were thought to have "strong medicine" that allowed the soldiers to shoot them straighter and farther than others. When the time came to fight, these great warriors carried those arrows and a sacred rope into battle, and just before the fight began, they would drive the rope into the ground with a stake. There were only two options from that moment on: fight until they could move the stake forward and the battle was done, or fight in place until they were done in by the competition. Retreat was not an option. It was not uncommon after a battle to find dead enemies in a semicircle around the Dog Soldiers.

For all this and more, the Dog Soldiers were held in the highest regard. Every child looked up to them. Tribesmen and elders alike respected them. Their power was indisputable, their virtue unquestionable, and their courage undeniable.

For more than 25 years, I have told this story to my sales and marketing teams and the people on the "front lines" in my own businesses and those I have worked for. In the days before I led us into a big presentation or the start of a huge initiative—true pivotal moments for the company—I gathered the team together and told them tales of those Dog Soldiers. I let them know I expected them to perform with the same excellence. They were the models for what we expected from one another—not the selfish athletes of today, but true heroes. My team and I were headed into "battle" where the competition had every intention of "killing" us. I wanted my team members to know how much the company and I were counting on them. They set the mood as our ambassadors for change and growth. And as with the Dog Soldiers, our survival in some ways depended on them.

At this point in my story, I stop and call out to those people who have honored us with their excellence in the past. I have no rope to give, but I tell them that they have earned what I do have: a handmade arrow to remind them of the fights they have won and the battle to come. The arrows come from a true Chippewa Indian I know in Minnesota. Like the arrows of the Dog Soldiers, the arrowhead is flint, and the shaft has either single-feather or three-feather fletching bound by sinew, just as they would have been long ago.

I say to them, "Let this arrow be a reminder to you of the enemies we shall slay, the people we will protect, and the students to whom we will give hope, because that is the work of a Dog Soldier!" I wanted people in the company to know the importance of what they do and what they have done. I wanted people on the team and throughout the company to tell stories about them and aspire to be like them. I wanted people, when they saw us walking by, to say, "There goes the sales and marketing team. There go the people we most look up to. There go our Dog Soldiers."

Say what you will about my flair for drama, the story works and is sacred to me. It has power and meaning. I know people who still have those arrows 25 years later—the same arrows I wish to "give" to everyone who has gotten to this point in the book. And like my challenge to my teams, I hand it to you while repeating the same challenge with which this book began: go!

Change is never easy, nor should it be. If it feels too easy, it is. So, stand proud, and remember the story of the Dog Soldiers. As they fought, the Dog Soldiers sang their own song in the face of death. This is the song of the change agent. Even as the proverbial bullets and arrows fly, even as you get hit from all sides, stand by your conditions of satisfaction and stand unwavering through all the "pain" again and again.

Others may run away; you can't. And when you succeed, no one will be held in higher regard. Get over the fear of change in your business and start acting. Fear is part of the game, but, unlike the Dog Soldiers, no one is going to die. You have my admiration and respect. See you on the other side of the gauntlet.

Enjoy the ride!

Twenty questions you must ask to win before you begin

My process for understanding value and asking questions is known as RACE (Research, Action, Communicate, Evaluate). These are the 20 RACE questions that you must ask to win before you begin:

1. What are you selling?

2. How much business or money is at stake?

3. Is the process repeatable or scalable?

4. What have you done to ensure that you can pull this off?

5. To whom are you selling?

6. Are you selling to those customers in the right way?

7. Are you charging what you should charge?

8. Are you focused on quality?

9. Can your target customers afford what you're selling?

10. What and how much analysis have you done to come to the conclusions and answer the questions asked so far?

11. What is your unique selling proposition (USP)?

12. What is your customers' connection to this USP and to what you are selling?

13. How do you compare to the competition in terms of what you are selling?

14. What will the competition do and say when you begin?

15. What will your customers and potential customers do or say when you begin?

16. What will your team do or say when you begin?

17. Have you given your team members the tools they need to succeed?

18. What could go wrong, and how have you prepared for that?

19. How will you measure your success?

20. When will the needle start moving?

My four social media Es for customer relations: engage, educate, excite, and evangelize.

Y ou may not think your customers are always right, but thanks to social media, they are now always in charge. Social media, e-mail, and intranets are the primary tools for connecting with and understanding your customers. The goal is to get your customers to talk about you—whether good or bad. The worst thing that can happen is that people say nothing about you. To get customers talking, follow my four Es.

ENGAGE

Social media gives everyone a potentially powerful platform, and each person is connected to other people who could be your customers, so be prepared to engage them all. And engagement means actually *engaging*—regularly. Regardless of your company's size, the more you do, the bigger your responsibility to engage. Of the four Es, none of the others matter without this one. Every day, you must go to the screens and find out what people are saying about you. Engagement almost always leads to a chance to educate and create new relationships. The more you lead, the more they will follow.

EDUCATE

The ability to educate your customers in real time about why your product is better or excelling and what the benefits are is incredible. And if you are wrong and changes need to be made, you can tell your customers quickly and directly what you are going to do about the problem. If you can solve a customer's problem, then you and that customer will get excited about the process and your new one-to-one relationship.

EXCITE

Once you have engaged and educated your customers, you need to generate some kind of excitement to keep the majority of them coming back and sharing what you do with more of their connections and communities. Whether it is offering key information in a blog, a contest, a challenge, or just a chance to be a part of something, the more you give them a reason to keep coming back, the deeper the relationships.

EVANGELIZE

What your company is doing won't matter a lick if more and more people don't know about it, and no business can spread the word on its own. It needs evangelists. So, engage and make great impressions on your most active ambassadors through education and excitement, and your message will reach millions instantly. Your brand ambassadors will create social media reverberation. Not only will they post about you positively, but they will "go off" on unfair and negative criticism on your behalf—something that you can't do on your own without revealing your self-interest.

The seven adapt-or-die questions to learn what you don't know

Awareness is key. As a business owner, you must be obsessed with the things that might put you out of business. You must drive new processes and continuously make improvements to existing ones. You must avoid getting in that success "rut" and falling victim to hubris. You never want to say, "Why didn't we think of that?" This means you had no idea something was even possible—that's failing to know what you don't know and losing after you begin (as opposed to saying, "I had no idea that was coming," which is losing before you begin; you failed to ask specific questions about an existing product or service that was coming to market because you moved too quickly or thought sloppily).

To uncover what you don't know, ask yourself these questions about your business:

1. Are you still relevant today?

2. What might change?

3. Are you acting deliberately and decisively to confront the realities of reaching today's customer?

4. Why do you do things the way you do them—do you use your own processes?

5. How do other people do what you do?

6. Are there other ways to approach the problems that you solve and the value that you deliver?

7. Are you moving quickly to bring new products and services to market faster, and are your response times as fast?

Index

About the Author

Jeffrey Hayzlett is a global business celebrity and former Fortune 100 c-suite executive. From small business to international corporations, he puts his creativity and extraordinary entrepreneurial skills into play, launching ventures blending his leadership perspectives, insights into professional development, mass marketing prowess, and affinity for social media.

Jeffrey is a leading business expert, cited in numerous books, magazines, and newspapers worldwide, and a frequent television guest and commentator, having appeared on shows including MSNBC's *Your Business*, Fox Business News, and NBC's *Celebrity Apprentice with Donald Trump*. He's executive producer of a number of global television projects. With a strong following in business and social media communities, he's recognized as one of the Top 10 c-suite Twitterers and a key influencer in the social media landscape.

Jeffrey is the author of the must-read business book *The Mirror Test*, which received acclaim on numerous bestseller lists, including the *Wall Street Journal, Inc Magazine,* and the *USA Today*. From the world of academia at leading business schools to corporate training and c-level circles, *The Mirror Test's* thought-provoking lessons are told with bold simplicity, readability, and humor. Christie Hefner, former CEO of Playboy Enterprises, says *The Mirror Test* "provide(s) fresh insights and actionable advice in an engaging style."

Not only engaging through his writing, Jeffrey's presence and insight is in demand; he frequently appears at events worldwide, addressing business growth, communications, and marketing. He has won numerous awards and honors and has been inducted into the Sales & Marketing Executives International Hall of Fame Academy of Achievement and into the Business Marketing Hall of Fame.

Jeffrey currently sits on numerous corporate and company boards of directors. In addition, he sits on the Business Marketing Association (BMA) board of directors, is a past chairman of BMA, a member of the advisory board of the CMO Council, chairman of the Sales and Marketing Executives International (SMEI) Foundation for Marketing Education, a permanent trustee of the SMEI Academy of Achievement Sales and Marketing Hall of Fame, and a two-term past chairman of SMEI. Jeffrey remains a trustee of Pi Sigma Epsilon National Education Foundation, an international sales and marketing fraternity. As celebrity editor of *Tweeting & Business* Magazine, Jeffrey lends his social media prowess and c-suite status to the innovative leading business publication.

Currently, Jeffrey leads The Hayzlett Group, an international strategic business consulting company leading change for high-growth businesses. Drawing upon an eclectic background in business, buoyed by a stellar track record of keynote speaking, and deeply rooted in cowboy lore, Jeffrey energizes his role driving and delivering change. He is a turnaround architect of the highest order, a maverick marketer who delivers scalable campaigns, embraces traditional modes of customer engagement, and possesses a remarkable cachet of mentorship, corporate governance, and brand building. Even when away from his home state of South Dakota, Jeffrey can always be found in his trademark cowboy boots.

When not traveling, Jeffrey lives in New York and Sioux Falls.